Jill Dupleix
very simplefood

notes

All spoon measures are level; 1 tsp = 5 ml spoon; 1 tbsp = 15 ml spoon. All eggs are free-range and large; all herbs are fresh; all salt is sea salt, and all pepper is freshly ground black pepper unless otherwise stated. All recipe ideas serve 4 unless otherwise suggested.

Creative Director Mary Evans
Project Editor Janet Illsley
Production Phil Dauncey

First published in 2003 by
Quadrille Publishing Limited
Alhambra House
27-31 Charing Cross Road
London WC2H OLS

Text and photographs © Jill Dupleix
Design and layout © Quadrille
Publishing Limited

Cataloguing in Publication Data: a catalogue record for this book is available from the British Library.

ISBN 1 844000 32 X
Printed in China

www.jilldupleix.com

text and
photographs by
Jill Dupleix

quadrille

This book is all about everyday food; simple food that uses smart tricks. It's full of ideas for that chicken breast, fish fillet or bag of potatoes you just brought home. I've designed it to give you the food you need to survive the working week, and the food you love to share with friends on the weekend.

I like flavours that taste fresh and bright, recipes that don't make you nervous, and food that is healthy enough to keep us out of the clutches of diet fads and self-help gurus. But the real secret to very simple food is very good produce. Shop well, and you will cook well.

I also think it's time to rethink some of the conventions of the day. Why must a 'proper' meal be made up of three courses, instead of a tableful of small and interesting dishes ready to share? If we really love cheese or salad, why don't we make them the heart of the meal rather than something tacked on at the end when we're too full to enjoy them? Why don't we picnic inside, and take our dining table outdoors? I have no idea why not.

I don't make my own pastry, refuse to deep-fry, won't stone olives, and will never be found peeling grapes. I also believe it's perfectly acceptable to cheat at cooking as long as you don't kill anyone.

The trick is to keep things simple, for ourselves and our food. Very simple.

Jill

starters

Cucumber 'sandwiches'

This is a blindingly simple and endlessly flexible idea for all you canapé crusaders out there. Cucumber rounds give you freshness and crunch, and carry all manner of sympathetic flavours, such as smoked salmon (featured here), smoked trout, fresh prawns or crab.

Peel the cucumber lengthwise, leaving a few thin strips of skin for a decorative effect. Cut the cucumber into 1cm slices – you should get around 32 slices.

Arrange half the cucumber slices on a board. Dab a little horseradish sauce on each one to help the salmon stay in one place. Cut the smoked salmon into 16 pieces, fold loosely and arrange on top of the cucumber slices on the board. Season with salt and pepper.

Cover with another cucumber slice. Add a little dab of horseradish sauce and top with a parsley leaf and a salted caper, then serve.

MAKES 16

1 long cucumber

2 tbsp horseradish sauce

150 g thinly sliced smoked
    salmon

sea salt

freshly ground black pepper

16 flat-leaf parsley sprigs

16 salted capers

Lemon mussels

Why serve mussels out of their shells when the shells can double as perfect little appetiser plates? Do this as a big party platter, or as elegant individual first courses.

Discard any broken mussels, and those that do not close when sharply tapped. Scrub the mussels well and pull out the little beards. Put the wine, parsley stems and garlic in a large lidded pan and bring to the boil. Add the mussels, cover with the lid and cook for 1 minute, then shake the pan, remove lid and take out the mussels as they open. Repeat this process, discarding any mussels that don't open.

Let the mussels cool to room temperature, then discard the top half-shells, saving four. Arrange the mussels on platters. Mix the preserved lemon with the parsley, olive oil and lemon juice. Spoon a little lemony dressing onto each mussel in the half-shell.

Beat the mayonnaise with the paprika and spoon into the reserved shells for dipping. Put one on each platter and serve.

SERVES 4
1.5 kg black mussels
250 ml dry white wine
handful of parsley stems
2 garlic cloves, squashed
2 tbsp finely chopped
preserved lemon
2 tbsp finely chopped parsley
2 tbsp extra virgin olive oil
1 tbsp lemon juice
2 tbsp quality mayonnaise
$\frac{1}{2}$ tsp paprika

soy roasted nuts

Soy roasted nuts

This simple technique not only freshens up mixed nuts, it coats them with a lightly crunchy, seductively sweet-salty flavour. Tamari is a wheat-free soy sauce, available in Asian stores and helpful supermarkets.

Heat the oven to 180°C/Gas 4. Line the base of a roasting tray with a sheet of foil, scatter the nuts on the foil and roast for 10 minutes, tossing them occasionally.

Mix the tamari and sugar in a bowl. Remove the tray from the oven and tip the nuts into the bowl, tossing until well coated. Using a slotted spoon, return the nuts to the foil-lined tray. Roast for up to 10 minutes until they are dry, tossing every minute or so and watching carefully to ensure they don't burn.

Leave the roasted nuts on the tray until they are completely cool, then store in an airtight jar until needed. Serve with drinks, or scattered through salads.

MAKES 500g

500g mixed shelled nuts
   (eg blanched almonds,
   brazil nuts, hazelnuts,
   pistachios)
100ml tamari or soy sauce
1 tbsp caster sugar

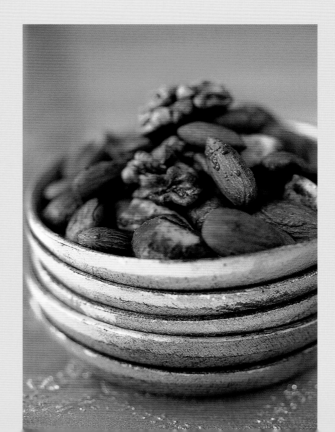

Smoked salmon martini

Save on making cocktail snacks for your next party, by putting the cocktail snack in the cocktail. First, you sip the vodka martini, then you eat the vodka-marinated smoked salmon and the olive. Then you have another one.

First, chill four martini glasses until they are frosty. Cut the smoked salmon slices in half lengthwise, twist each piece into a spiral and place in the glasses.

Pour the vodka and dry vermouth over ice into a shaker, stir well and strain into the glasses. Add a green olive to each glass and serve.

MAKES 4
2 thin slices smoked salmon
300 ml vodka
60 ml dry vermouth
4 green or stuffed olives

Parmesan biscuits

These rich, cheesy little biscuits make the perfect nibble with drinks. Send out a stack with a tray of icy cold dry martinis, or tall, frosty glasses of chilled white wine, or serve them with little cups of creamy vegetable soup.

Heat the oven to 180°C/Gas 4. Cut the butter into small dice. Put the butter, flour, cheese, sea salt, pepper and cayenne in the food processor and whiz until sandy. Add the iced water and whiz again until the dough is moist and clumpy. Add extra water if necessary.

Form into a ball, roll out to 1 cm thickness on a lightly floured bench, and cut into 5 cm rounds. Place on a non-stick baking tray, brush lightly with beaten egg, and scatter with thyme and rosemary.

Bake for 10 to 12 minutes or until lightly golden, then transfer to a wire rack to cool. Store in an airtight container for up to 2 weeks.

MAKES 12

100 g butter, chilled

150 g plain flour

80 g parmesan, cheddar or
    gruyère, grated

½ tsp sea salt

freshly ground black pepper

pinch of cayenne pepper

1 tbsp iced water

1 free-range egg, beaten

1 tbsp thyme and rosemary
    leaves

Thai corn cakes

Crisp, golden little fritters that practically pop in the mouth with juicy corn kernels. Stack high and drizzle with sweet, seedy Thai chilli sauce.

Whiz half the sweetcorn in a blender to a purée. Pound the garlic, shallots and coriander stalks until smashed. Add to the blender with the sugar, fish sauce, salt and pepper, and whiz to a purée.

Add the flour and whiz for 1 minute, then add the eggs and process for another 30 seconds. Tip into a bowl and fold through the remaining sweetcorn, reserving 1 tbsp for serving.

Heat the oil in a heavy-based frying pan until it starts to smoke. Drop 4 tablespoonfuls of batter into the pan, spacing them apart, and cook until golden, turning once. Remove and drain on paper towels. Keep warm while you make the remaining cakes.

Scatter with corn kernels and spring onions, and drizzle with sweet chilli sauce to serve.

MAKES 16

275g canned sweetcorn
kernels, drained
2 garlic cloves, peeled
2 shallots, peeled
2 coriander stalks
1 tsp caster sugar
1 tbsp Thai fish sauce
1 tsp sea salt
1/2 tsp freshly ground
black pepper
100g plain flour
2 large free-range eggs
2 tbsp vegetable oil,
for frying
2 spring onions, finely chopped
100ml sweet chilli sauce

party sushi

Party sushi

Make these just before guests arrive and keep in an airtight container, or turn the making of them into a party piece, and keep them rolling out to order. Party, or temaki sushi are light, fresh and healthy, and fun to eat in your hands. Add cooked prawns, sashimi-quality tuna or avocado, as you see fit.

MAKES 20

Sushi rice:

60 ml rice vinegar

2 tbsp caster sugar

1 tsp salt

400g sushi rice

500 ml water

To assemble:

½ cucumber

1 sweet red pepper

1 sweet yellow pepper

2 tsp wasabi powder

1 tbsp quality mayonnaise

20 sheets nori (toasted seaweed sheet)

250g thinly sliced smoked salmon

To make the sushi rice dressing, gently heat the rice vinegar, sugar and salt in a small pan until the sugar has dissolved, then cool.

Wash the rice in a sieve under cold running water, drain well, tip into a saucepan and add the water. Bring to the boil, cover tightly and simmer very gently for 15 minutes. Turn off the heat and leave for another 10 minutes undisturbed, then turn the rice out onto a baking sheet or tray.

Sprinkle the rice with the cooled dressing, tossing it well with a wooden spoon to cool it quickly. Keep the rice covered with a damp cloth until ready to use, which should be the same day.

Cut the cucumber and sweet peppers into thin batons or strips, discarding the pepper core and seeds. Mix the wasabi powder to a paste with the mayonnaise.

Place a heaped tablespoonful of sushi rice on the left-hand side of a sheet of nori. Add a dab of wasabi mayonnaise, a small fold of smoked salmon, some cucumber, and red and yellow pepper strips, and roll from left to right into a cone shape. A few grains of rice will help the final flap stick. Eat in the hands.

Tuna with sesame soy

Really fresh tuna has a pure, sweet flavour and melt-in-the-mouth texture. This no-cook, no-fuss, first course makes the most of tuna by teaming it with soy sauce, sesame oil and mirin (sweet rice wine), available from Japanese food stores and helpful supermarkets.

Trim the tuna of all bloodlines and cut into a neat shape to enable you to cut it into small dice, around 1cm. Discard any obvious sinews or icky bits.

Whisk the soy sauce, mirin, sesame oil and mustard together in a bowl. Add the tuna and toss lightly to coat in the dressing.

Mix the rice vinegar and olive oil with sea salt and pepper in a second bowl. Pick the leaves from the watercress, toss in the dressing, then arrange on four serving plates.

Pile the tuna in little pyramids on top of the leaves, and scatter with finely snipped chives. Serve with chopsticks.

SERVES 4

350g fresh sashimi-quality tuna

1 tbsp soy sauce

1 tbsp mirin

1 tsp sesame oil

$\frac{1}{2}$ tsp Dijon mustard

1 tsp rice vinegar

1 tbsp olive oil

sea salt

freshly ground black pepper

100g watercress

1 tbsp finely snipped chives

Smoked salmon rolls

These glamorous rolls fulfil my three main criteria for easy entertaining: they take only minutes to make; can be done ahead of time; and they look a million dollars. Serve as a sit-down first course, or with drinks.

Beat 1 tbsp horseradish into the mascarpone. Gradually add the rest to taste – until the horseradish cream is hot enough for you. Add the chives, sea salt and pepper and fold them through the cream. (You can make this beforehand and refrigerate it.)

Trim the smoked salmon into 8 strips, each 15 x 5 cm. Place a spoonful of the horseradish cream on one end of each strip and roll up. It doesn't matter if the edges are a bit ragged.

MAKES 8

2 tbsp hot horseradish sauce

450g mascarpone or crème fraîche

2 tbsp finely snipped chives, plus extra to serve

sea salt

freshly ground black pepper

250g thinly sliced smoked salmon

Sit each smoked salmon roll on its end, and scatter extra chives on the exposed cream at the top. (You can even do this an hour or two beforehand and refrigerate until required.) Serve one or two salmon rolls per person.

Salami tarts

I had some leftover pastry and salami, so I did the only thing possible – I made salami tarts, chilled a bottle of Spanish sherry and invited people around for a drink. The softer and fresher the salami – look for a Venetian-style soppressa – the better the tart.

Heat the oven to 200°C / Gas 6. Roll out the pastry thinly. Remove the skin from the salami slices. Place one salami slice on the pastry and cut around it, leaving a 1 cm border of pastry. Use this as your size guide for cutting out 10 identical pastry circles.

Brush each pastry round with beaten egg and top with a slice of salami. Bake for 10 minutes or until the pastry borders are puffy and golden. Transfer to a wire rack – they will crisp as they cool.

To cook the Swiss chard, wash it well and place in a saucepan with just the water clinging to the leaves. Cover and cook over high heat, tossing occasionally, until the leaves wilt and the juices evaporate. Set aside to cool, and squeeze out excess water. Toss in olive oil, with sea salt and lots of pepper.

Serve the salami tarts at room temperature, topped with a little mound of wilted Swiss chard.

MAKES 10
500g ready-rolled frozen
puff pastry, thawed
12 slices salami, around
6cm diameter
1 free-range egg, beaten
200g Swiss chard leaves
(silverbeet)
1 tbsp extra virgin olive oil
sea salt
freshly ground black pepper

party

Americano Pour 30 ml Campari Bitter and 15 ml sweet vermouth over ice in a chilled glass and top with soda water. Add a squeeze and a slice of orange. Serve with potato crisps and tiny finger sandwiches of prosciutto.

Anchovy sticks Cut 400 g ready-rolled puff pastry into long sticks and brush with tomato purée. Thinly slice 12 canned anchovy fillets lengthwise, arrange on top and brush with oil from the can. Dust with pepper and paprika and bake at 200°C/Gas 6 for 10 minutes. Serve warm.

Coriander orange olives Gently heat 2 tbsp olive oil with 2 finely sliced garlic cloves, 1 finely sliced red chilli, 6 rosemary sprigs, 6 thyme leaves, 2 bay leaves, 1 tbsp grated orange rind, 1 tbsp coriander seeds and 1 tsp fennel seeds. Add 450 g mixed olives, toss well and let cool.

Avocado, chive and lemon dip Whiz the flesh of 1 ripe avocado with 1 crushed garlic clove, 2 tbsp chopped parsley, 1 tbsp snipped chives, 2 tbsp lemon juice, 2 tbsp yoghurt, sea salt and pepper. Chill. Scatter with chives and serve with corn chips, rice crackers, grissini, or flat bread.

Lemon and smoked salmon dip Whiz 60 g smoked salmon with 200 g cream cheese, 100 ml yoghurt, 2 tsp horseradish cream, 1 tbsp lemon juice and lots of black pepper. Scatter with snipped chives or salmon roe, and serve with warm pitta, crispbread or crackers for dipping.

Things to dip Crisp leaves of witlof or cos, corn chips, grissini (crisp bread rusks), asparagus spears, green beans, prawns, celery sticks, cubes of feta cheese on cocktail sticks, flat bread, baby blinis, potato crisps, Japanese rice crackers, Chinese prawn crackers, Scandinavian crispbread.

Prosciutto grissini Wrap thinly sliced prosciutto (or smoked salmon) around one end of a crisp grissini rusk. Plonk the grissini in a tall glass or vase with a few stalks of rosemary, and serve soon after wrapping or the grissini will soften.

Party tapas Buy up big at a Spanish food store, and put together little toasts of jamon (cured ham) with membrillo (quince paste), manchego cheese, roasted sweet red peppers, anchovy fillets, prawns and sizzled slices of chorizo, in any combination. Serve with chilled sherry.

Tuna sticks with lemon soy Find 500g very fresh sashimi-quality tuna and cut into neat 2cm cubes. Pierce each cube with a cocktail stick, and dip the tuna into white sesame seeds or spicy Japanese pepper. Serve with a dipping sauce of 100ml soy sauce and 1 tbsp lemon juice.

Pesto toasts Cut 200g cherry tomatoes in half, and bake at 180°C/ Gas 4 for 20 minutes. Cut white bread into little squares, place in the turned-off oven until crisp. Cool the toasts, top with a spoonful of pesto and an oven-roasted cherry tomato, add sea salt and pepper and serve.

Champagne gelati Drop two scoops of your favourite store-bought gelato (eg lemon, raspberry) into well chilled champagne flutes and top with chilled Champagne – do this very slowly, or it will froth up and over the glass. Serve icy cold.

Beyond the canapé Put all your money into a 2kg wedge of aged Parmigiano Reggiano cheese, surround it with crusty bread, finely shaved celery, olives and anchovies, and let people help themselves.

prosciutto grissini

salads

Carrot and orange salad

A crisp, refreshing salad, this glows with warm, sweet spices and almost fluorescent sunny colours. It's perfect for a warm day, when you can scatter sliced summer radishes over the top. It's also perfect for a cold day, when it brings sunshine and the bite of winter's oranges to a meal of grilled fish, chicken or lamb.

SERVES 6

450g carrots

1 orange

handful of coriander and mint
leaves

Dressing:

2 tbsp orange juice

1 tbsp lemon juice

2 tbsp extra virgin olive oil

sea salt

freshly ground black pepper

1/2 tsp ground cumin

1/2 tsp ground cinnamon

1 tsp icing sugar

Peel the carrots and grate them coarsely. Peel the orange with a knife, removing all white pith. Cut it crosswise into 1 cm thick slices, then into small segments.

Whisk the dressing ingredients together in a large bowl. Add the grated carrot, orange segments, and coriander and mint leaves. Toss lightly to serve.

Bacon and tomato salad

This could be too simple for some, but I love putting fresh salads centre stage and making a meal of them. That way, I can eat my favourite foods, such as crisp bacon, without going overboard on them. Turn this salad into a meal with some pan-fried haloumi cheese, chicken livers, or one of Terry's fried eggs (page 136).

To make the dressing, combine the olive oil, vinegar, mustard, sea salt and pepper in a large bowl and whisk well until combined. Cut half of the cherry tomatoes in half and marinate in the dressing.

Grill the bacon under a preheated grill on both sides until crisp. Drain on paper towels and cut into thick batons.

Wash and spin the leaves dry, then toss in the dressing with the marinated tomatoes and the whole tomatoes. Add the bacon and toss lightly, then distribute among four dinner plates and serve.

SERVES 4
200 g cherry tomatoes
4 rashers streaky bacon
200 g wild rocket or other salad leaves

Dressing:
2 tbsp extra virgin olive oil
1 tbsp red wine vinegar
1 tsp Dijon mustard
sea salt
freshly ground black pepper

feta tomato salad

Feta tomato salad

Turn a block of creamy feta cheese into food for the gods with a Greek chorus of chilli, olives, herbs and good olive oil. Serve with drinks, scatter over salads, take on picnics, or serve alongside a lazy al fresco lunch.

Finely slice the chilli into rings and place in a bowl with the olives, rosemary and oregano. Add the olive oil and pepper and stir to combine. (You won't need salt, as feta is quite salty.)

Rinse the feta, pat dry and place in a dish. Pour the marinade on top, cover and leave overnight, or at least for a few hours.

Lift the feta out of the marinade and arrange on a serving plate in its original blocks, or cut into bite-sized cubes. Cut the tomatoes in half, add to the marinade to coat lightly, then spoon over the feta. Serve with crusty bread.

SERVES 4 TO 6

1 small red chilli

2 tbsp kalamata olives

5 rosemary sprigs

1 tsp dried oregano

125 ml extra virgin olive oil

freshly ground black pepper

400 g good feta cheese

200 g cherry or baby plum
  tomatoes

Warm spring salad

A fresh, light, warm salad that fills the kitchen with spring-like aromas. Use fresh peas and broad beans in season, or frozen ones out of season – they're perfectly acceptable.

Cook the potatoes in simmering salted water for about 15 minutes until tender. Cook the peas, broad beans and green beans in a separate pan of simmering salted water (with the shallots to make peeling easier) until tender, about 5 minutes. Drain, refresh in cold water and set aside. Pick out the shallots, peel and finely slice.

Heat half the olive oil in a fry pan and gently cook the shallots for 2 minutes. Add the peas and beans and toss to heat through. Drain the potatoes, cut in half on the diagonal and add to the pan. Take off the heat, add remaining olive oil, vinegar, salt and pepper, and toss well.

Scatter the rocket on four warmed plates and top with the beans, peas and potatoes. Drizzle with any remaining dressing and serve.

SERVES 4

12 waxy potatoes (eg kipfler, pink fir apple)

sea salt

450g fresh peas, podded

450g fresh broad beans, podded

250g fine green beans, trimmed

3 shallots (small, red onions)

3 tbsp extra virgin olive oil

2 tbsp red wine vinegar

freshly ground black pepper

150g baby rocket leaves or cress

Warm lentil salad

The great thing about these lentils and their pushy little tomato and mint dressing is that they go with anything. Serve them as a salad, as a meal with a fried egg on top, or with roast chicken. The best lentils are the slate-green French 'lentilles de Puy', available from good food stores.

Rinse the lentils and place in a saucepan with the onion, garlic, bay leaves and 1 litre cold water. Bring to the boil, then reduce the heat and simmer gently for 20 minutes or until the lentils are just tender. Drain thoroughly.

To make the dressing, cut the tomatoes in half, discard the juice and seeds, then chop the flesh. In a bowl, combine the chopped tomato with the mint, parsley, sea salt, pepper, extra virgin olive oil and red wine vinegar.

Toss the still-warm drained lentils in the tomato dressing, and divide between four salad plates. Serve warm.

SERVES 4
250g green or brown lentils
1 onion, finely chopped
2 garlic cloves, smashed
2 bay leaves

Dressing:
2 tomatoes
2 tbsp chopped mint
1 tbsp roughly chopped
 flat-leaf parsley
sea salt
freshly ground black pepper
2 tbsp extra virgin olive oil
1 tbsp red wine vinegar

Torn mozzarella and peppers

I fell in love with this torn salad at Geoff Lindsay's opalescent Pearl restaurant in Melbourne, Australia. It looks like a bottomless pizza, and should be served with crusty bread or warmed flat bread. Fresh buffalo milk mozzarella is heavenly. If you can't find it, you could use good feta or fresh ricotta.

Holding the peppers upright, cut the 'sides' away from the core and seeds, then cut each piece into 1cm squares.

Combine the peppers with the olive oil, sea salt and pepper in a saucepan and stew gently over a low heat for 10 to 15 minutes, without allowing them to 'fry' or brown. Remove from the heat and leave to cool until barely warm.

To serve, set out four dinner plates or one very large platter. Using a slotted spoon, arrange the peppers over the plate, saving the oil. Tear the parsley leaves into shreds with your fingers and scatter over the top.

Drain the mozzarella and pat dry. Tear the soft, fresh cheese into small bits with your fingers, discarding any thick skin, and dot around the plate at random. Drizzle with the reserved oil to serve.

SERVES 4
2 sweet red peppers
2 sweet yellow peppers
2 tbsp extra virgin olive oil
sea salt
freshly ground black pepper
2 tbsp flat-leaf parsley
2 fresh mozzarella bocconcini
(balls), each about 125g

Spanish café salad

Every country with a café culture does a great café salad – a loose, casual combination of readily available produce. This is my idea of a Spanish café salad, using Spain's beautiful serrano ham. It's extremely flexible – you could use prosciutto instead of jamon, add some fresh goat cheese, or drop the artichoke hearts to make it your own.

SERVES 4

150g fine green beans, trimmed
250g asparagus, trimmed
salt
2 tomatoes
½ cucumber
200g mixed salad leaves (eg little gem or baby cos lettuce, rocket, frisée)
8 small artichoke hearts, preserved in oil
2 tbsp olives
12 thin slices serrano ham (jamon)

Dressing:
2 tbsp extra virgin olive oil
1 tbsp sherry or red wine vinegar
sea salt
freshly ground black pepper

Cook the green beans and asparagus in simmering salted water for 4 minutes. Drain and cool under cold running water, then drain again.

Cut the tomatoes into quarters, or eighths if large. Peel the cucumber, halve lengthwise and slice finely.

To make the dressing, whisk the ingredients together in a large bowl. Toss the leaves, green beans and asparagus in the dressing and arrange on four dinner plates. Toss the tomatoes, cucumber, artichoke hearts and olives in any remaining dressing and scatter them freely over the leaves.

Using a fork, pull a few of the buried leaves to the surface. Drape the slices of serrano ham on top of the salad and serve.

japanese salmon with mirin

Japanese salmon with mirin

A light, fresh, tangy salad that's as cool as a cucumber on a warm summer's day or evening. If you think there are too many combinations of salmon and cucumber in this book, you're probably right, but I find the two irresistible.

Score the skin of the cucumber lengthwise with the tines of a fork, then slice finely. Combine the lime or lemon juice, rice vinegar, mirin, sea salt, pepper, sugar and chives in a bowl and stir until the sugar has dissolved. Add the cucumber slices, toss to coat and set aside until ready to serve.

Heat the oil in a non-stick fry pan and sear the salmon fillets on both sides until almost cooked through, but still pink in the centre. Allow to cool, then divide into bite-sized flakes with your fingers.

Drain the cucumber slices, reserving the liquid. Arrange in small mounds on four dinner plates and top with the flaked salmon. Whisk the olive oil with 2 tbsp of the cucumber dressing, salt and pepper, and spoon over and around the salmon.

SERVES 4

1 cucumber

1 tbsp lime or lemon juice

1 tbsp rice vinegar

1 tbsp mirin (Japanese rice wine)

sea salt

freshly ground black pepper

1 tsp caster sugar

2 tbsp finely snipped chives

1 tbsp vegetable oil

450 g fresh salmon fillets

2 tbsp olive oil

Chicken Waldorf

The real reason I lightened up the famous salad of apple, celery and walnuts from The Waldorf Astoria in New York is so I can eat more of it. Do this when you have a crowd to feed for Sunday lunch.

Rinse the chicken and place in a wide, shallow pan. Cover with cold water, add the bay leaf and onion half, and bring to just below the boil. Skim off any froth, and simmer gently for 15 minutes, then cover, turn off the heat and leave to steep for 30 minutes. Drain and allow to cool. (You can prepare to this point in advance, although the chicken will be nicer if it isn't refrigerated.)

To make the dressing, whisk the mayonnaise, yoghurt, apple juice, lemon juice, salt and pepper together in a bowl.

Lightly toast the walnuts in a hot, dry pan for a couple of minutes. Remove any strings from the celery, then finely slice. Quarter and core the apples, then dice finely. Add to the dressing with the celery, walnuts and dill, and toss well.

Finely slice the chicken, add to the salad and toss lightly. Arrange the lettuce leaves on eight dinner plates or one large buffet plate, and spoon the salad on top.

SERVES 8
4 chicken breasts
1 bay leaf
1/2 onion
2 tbsp walnuts, roughly chopped
4 celery sticks
2 red or green skinned apples
2 tbsp finely chopped fresh dill
crisp lettuce leaves to serve

Dressing:
1 tbsp quality mayonnaise
1 tbsp natural yoghurt
2 tbsp apple juice
1 tsp lemon juice
sea salt
freshly ground black pepper

Fig and radicchio salad

When figs are in season, I keep trying to find new ways of eating them so that I can fit more in. This salad combines the rich, warm colours of ripe purple figs, pink prosciutto and ruby-toned radicchio leaves with the crunch of fennel and freshness of mint.

Separate the radicchio leaves, then tear each one roughly in two or three. Very finely slice the fennel bulb crosswise. Quarter the figs.

In a large bowl, whisk the dressing ingredients together. Lightly toss the radicchio leaves, sliced fennel and mint leaves in the dressing, then arrange on four dinner plates.

Arrange the figs on top, and tuck in the slices of prosciutto. Roughly chop or pinch the cheese into sections and scatter over the top. Drizzle any remaining dressing over the salad and serve, with Italian grissini (rusks) or crusty bread.

SERVES 4

2 heads radicchio, trimmed

1 fennel bulb, trimmed

4 ripe figs

20 mint leaves

8 thin slices prosciutto

150g fresh ricotta or goat cheese

Dressing:

2 tbsp extra virgin olive oil

1 tbsp balsamic vinegar

1 tsp cold water

sea salt

freshly ground black pepper

lunch

Pitta pockets

This is my very simple version of an Italian snack made with piadina, a soft, unleavened bread from Emiglia-Romana. I use Greek pitta bread instead, stuffing it with prosciutto, rocket and mozzarella, then warming it until the cheese goes gooey.

Heat the oven to 180°C/Gas 4. Toss the rocket leaves in the olive oil with sea salt and pepper. Drain the mozzarella and slice thinly. Cut the sun-dried tomatoes in half.

Cut or tear the pitta breads in half and gently work them open to form pockets. Stuff each pocket with rocket leaves, prosciutto, sun-dried tomatoes and mozzarella, until quite full. If the bread splits at the side, just wrap in foil to keep it together.

MAKES 4

100g rocket leaves

1 tbsp extra virgin olive oil

sea salt

freshly ground black pepper

2 fresh mozzarella bocconcini (balls), each about 125g

4 sun-dried tomatoes in oil

4 pitta breads

8 slices prosciutto

2 tbsp pesto

Place the stuffed pittas on a tray and heat through in the oven for 4 to 5 minutes, or until the cheese melts. (Or you can warm them on a medium-hot barbecue or griddle for just a few minutes, turning once, until the cheese melts.) Don't heat them for too long, or the bread will turn brittle.

Drizzle a generous teaspoonful of pesto into each stuffed pitta and serve two halves to each person.

Greek stack

A new angle on everyone's favourite Greek salad – serve it stacked high on warm pitta bread. If you want something meatier for lunch, add some spiced grilled lamb or a few garlicky sausages to the side.

Discard the outer cos leaves, then cut the lettuce crosswise into 4 thick, chunky rounds. Thickly slice the tomatoes and season with sea salt and pepper. Cut the feta into 4 chunky slices. Halve the anchovy fillets lengthwise.

To make the dressing, whisk the extra virgin olive oil, lemon juice, sea salt and pepper in a bowl. Add the olives and toss to coat.

Gently warm the pitta bread in a warm oven or on the grill, and place on four warmed dinner plates. Top each pitta with a layer of tomatoes, then a round of cos lettuce, followed by the feta, another slice of tomato, and a few onion rings. Top with anchovy strips and spoon the dressing and olives over the lot.

SERVES 4

1 cos (romaine) lettuce

4 ripe tomatoes

sea salt

freshly ground black pepper

400 g good feta cheese

4 anchovy fillets

3 tbsp extra virgin olive oil

1 tbsp lemon juice

2 tbsp kalamata or small black olives

4 small pitta breads

1 onion, very finely sliced

baked scotch eggs

Salmon egg tarts

This is a sequel to the little ham and egg pies that appeared in Simple Food. Muffin moulds are filled with fresh salmon, cream, curry powder and a whole egg, and baked to produce effortless, pastryless tarts.

Heat the oven to 160°C/Gas 3. Lightly oil or butter a 12-hole muffin tray. Finely chop the raw or cooked salmon and place in a bowl. Add the cream, curry powder, sea salt, pepper, and dill or chives, and mix lightly with a fork.

Divide the salmon mixture between the moulds, then break an egg into each mould. Using a fork, jiggle the egg white so that it mixes with some of the salmon, leaving the yolk whole.

Bake for 20 to 25 minutes until set. Leave to cool for 5 minutes, then run a knife around each mould to loosen, and remove the egg tarts to a wire tray.

Scatter with dill or chives and eat warm or at room temperature. Serve one as a starter with drinks, two with a salad for lunch, or take the lot on a picnic.

MAKES 12

1 tsp olive oil or butter

400g salmon fillet, raw or
   cooked

2 tbsp single cream

1 tsp curry powder

1/2 tsp sea salt

freshly ground black pepper

2 tbsp finely chopped dill or
   snipped chives, plus extra
   to serve

12 free-range eggs

Baked Scotch eggs

Because I don't deep-fry, I've invented other ways of having my favourite foods. These Scotch eggs are baked in a muffin tray, in a wrap of bacon. No crumbing, no deep-frying. Simple, really.

Heat the oven to 190°C/Gas 5. Lightly oil a 12-hole muffin tray. Put the eggs in a large pan of hot water, bring to the boil and simmer for 5 minutes from the moment the water starts to bubble. Immediately drain and run under cold water to stop further cooking; cool and peel.

Soak the bread in the milk for 1 minute. Drain and squeeze dry. Combine the bread and sausagemeat in a bowl, using your hands. Add the beaten egg, parsley, nutmeg, salt and pepper and mix well.

Line each muffin mould with a bacon rasher. Press some meat into the base. Add the egg, pointy end up, and pack the meat around and over the egg to cover completely. Bake for 20 minutes until nicely browned. Leave in the moulds for 10 minutes. Drain off any juices, run a knife around to loosen and serve hot, warm or cold.

MAKES 12
1 tsp vegetable oil
12 large free-range eggs
5 slices white sandwich bread, crusts removed
200 ml milk
1 kg good sausagemeat (eg veal and pork)
1 free-range egg, beaten
1 tbsp chopped parsley
$\frac{1}{2}$ tsp ground nutmeg
sea salt
freshly ground black pepper
12 rindless rashers streaky bacon

paprika salmon

Chilli lime chicken wings

Thai flavours – garlic, lime juice, coriander and chilli – give chicken wings a boost, turning them into an easy lunch. Serve with a sweet, sticky chilli and lime dipping sauce.

Cut off the tips of the chicken wings, and bend each wing until you can cut cleanly between the joints.

Roughly chop the coriander stalks and pound with the garlic, chilli, salt and sugar until you have a rough paste. Add the fish sauce, lime juice and oil, and stir well. Rub this marinade all over the chicken pieces and leave to marinate in the refrigerator for a couple of hours or overnight, turning once or twice.

Heat the oven to 220°C/Gas 7. Place the chicken on a foil-lined roasting tray and bake for 30 minutes until crisp and golden. Or grill on a ribbed cast-iron griddle or a barbecue, turning once.

To make the chilli lime sauce, heat the sugar, vinegar and sliced chilli in a saucepan, stirring until the sugar has dissolved. Bring to the boil and allow to bubble and reduce for a few minutes until the sauce is syrupy. Remove from the heat and add the lime juice, fish sauce and coriander leaves.

Drizzle the chicken wings with the chilli lime sauce and serve with lime quarters.

SERVES 4
8 medium chicken wings
4 coriander stalks
4 garlic cloves
1 small red or green chilli
1 tsp salt
1 tsp caster sugar
2 tbsp Thai fish sauce or
    soy sauce
2 tbsp lime juice
2 tbsp vegetable oil

Chilli lime sauce:
100g sugar
125ml white vinegar
1 small red chilli, sliced
2 tbsp lime juice
2 tbsp Thai fish sauce
2 tbsp coriander leaves

To serve:
lime quarters

Paprika salmon

This is a smart way of cooking salmon for a special lunch, spiking it with paprika oil and serving it simply, with roasted red peppers, capers and watercress.

Heat the oven to 220°C/Gas 7. Lightly oil the peppers and roast for 20 minutes until scorched. Transfer the peppers to a bowl, cover and set aside. Place a good, solid baking tray in the oven to heat up for 3 minutes.

Mix the olive oil with the paprika, sea salt and pepper, and coat the salmon with the spiced oil. Lightly oil the hot baking tray and place the salmon on it, skin-side down. Bake for 10 to 12 minutes, or until the salmon is still a little pink inside.

When the peppers are cool enough to handle, strip off the skin and cut the flesh into strips, discarding the core and seeds. Rinse the watercress, shake dry and discard the thicker stems.

To make the dressing, whisk the ingredients together, with salt and pepper, until slightly thickened. Toss the watercress in the dressing and place on warmed dinner plates. Lay the seared salmon, skin-side up, on the cress and arrange the peppers and capers on top.

SERVES 4
2 sweet red peppers
2 tbsp extra virgin olive oil, plus extra to oil peppers
1 tsp paprika
sea salt
freshly ground black pepper
6 thick salmon fillets, around 200g each
250g watercress
1 tbsp small capers, rinsed

Dressing:
2 tbsp extra virgin olive oil
1 tbsp lemon juice or red wine vinegar
1 tsp caster sugar

Fish in a bag

When you cook fish in a sealed foil bag, it retains all its delicacy and flavour. Add cherry tomatoes, spinach – or fine green beans or asparagus – and garlic to the bag and you get a complete meal with no mess, no fuss, and no loss of flavour.

Wash the spinach leaves well, rinse and shake dry. Heat the oven to 220°C/Gas 7. Cut out four 38cm squares of foil.

Divide the spinach leaves between the foil squares. Season the fish well with sea salt and pepper and place on the spinach. Toss the cherry tomatoes and garlic with the olive oil, salt and pepper, then spoon on top of the fish.

Bring two opposite sides of foil up to meet in the middle, and crimp tightly from the middle to the outer edge, shaping it into a half-moon as you go. Now fold the crimped edge over again, squeezing it tightly so air cannot escape. Bake for 15 minutes until the bag has puffed up like a balloon.

Snip open each parcel, drain off most of the juices, and slide the contents onto warm dinner plates. Drizzle with olive oil and serve with lemon wedges.

SERVES 4
250g spinach leaves
(grown-up, not baby)
4 thick white fish fillets
(eg cod, haddock,
snapper), each 180g
sea salt
freshly ground black pepper
200g cherry tomatoes
2 garlic cloves, thinly sliced
2 tbsp extra virgin olive oil,
plus extra to drizzle
1 lemon, quartered

Salt-grilled sardines

Long after the holiday bills have been paid and the suntan has faded, you can relive the memories of meals eaten by the sea or under the grapevines. These sardines take me right back to the smoky al fresco barbecues of the old Alfama district of Lisbon. And to think some people force themselves to eat oil-rich sardines and mackerel purely for their health.

SERVES 4

2 sweet red peppers

2 tbsp olive oil

8 large or 12 medium sardines, gutted, cleaned and scaled

1 tsp flaked sea salt (eg Maldon)

½ tsp freshly ground black pepper

pinch of cayenne pepper

a little extra virgin olive oil

1 lemon, quartered

Coat the sweet peppers with some of the olive oil and grill, turning occasionally, until scorched and blistered all over. Peel off the skin and cut the peppers into long strips, discarding the core and seeds.

Brush the sardines and the grill with oil to help prevent sticking. Roll the sardines in the sea salt, pepper and cayenne.

Grill or barbecue lightly on one side, then turn the sardines while they are still firm enough to be moved without breaking up. Grill or barbecue on the other side until the skin is scorched and bubbling.

Arrange the grilled sardines and peppers on serving plates. Add a drizzle of extra virgin olive oil and serve with a wedge of lemon.

bread

Cherry tomato bruschetta Toss 200g cherry tomatoes in 1 tbsp olive oil and bake at 180°C/Gas 4 for 20 minutes. Smash some garlic cloves in extra virgin olive oil, with sea salt and pepper. Grill 4 thick slices of sourdough bread, brush with the oil and top with the cherry tomatoes. Drizzle with more garlicky olive oil and serve.

Crostini with anchovies and capers Mash 8 canned anchovy fillets in oil with 1 tbsp rinsed capers, 1 tbsp finely chopped parsley and pepper. Mix to a paste, adding oil from the anchovy can, and spread on 2 big slices of grilled sourdough bread. Heat under the grill, then cut into fingers.

Turn soup into zuppa Grill thick slices of sourdough bread, brush with garlicky olive oil and place one slice in each bowl. Pour a simple vegetable and bean soup on top and serve. Try it scattered with grated cheese, too.

Cheat's pizza Spread 4 pitta, naan or Turkish flat breads with tomato salsa. Top with torn bocconcini (mozzarella balls), halved cherry tomatoes, anchovy fillets and dried oregano. Drizzle with extra virgin olive oil and bake at 180°C/Gas 4 for 8 minutes, or heat under the grill.

Crumbs! Mix 3 tbsp fresh breadcrumbs with 1 tbsp butter, 1 tsp lemon juice, $\frac{1}{2}$ tsp ground cumin, salt and pepper. Spoon onto mussels, oysters or sardines before grilling, or spread on fish or chicken fillets before roasting.

Little marmalade toasts Beat 200g mascarpone with 1 tbsp caster sugar, 1 tbsp bitter orange marmalade, and 1 tbsp Cointreau or whisky. Finely slice a baguette and grill lightly on both sides. Spread with a little marmalade, and top with the marmalade mascarpone. Serve with espresso coffee at a brunch party, or after dinner.

Peach bruschetta Cut a dry baguette into two 15cm long sections, split in half lengthwise, and lightly butter. Crush the flesh of 4 ripe peaches or 8 apricots onto the bread, scatter with raspberries and sprinkle with 1 tbsp caster sugar. Bake at 180°C/Gas 4 for 10 to 15 minutes until the bread is crisp. Dust with icing sugar and serve as a dessert with crème fraîche.

Baked feta bread Slash a long baguette (as for garlic bread). Crush 2 garlic cloves in 2 tbsp olive oil with a few rosemary sprigs. Cut 200g feta cheese into slices, coat in the oil and wedge into each cut. Wrap in foil and bake at 180°C/Gas 4 for 10 minutes until hot.

Prosciutto croissants Cut 4 large croissants in half, and lightly grill the cut sides. Cover with sliced prosciutto and top with sliced bocconcini (mozzarella balls). Grill briefly until the cheese is soft, and serve hot.

Italian bread salad Grill 2 thick slices of country style bread and cut into cubes. Combine with 1 finely chopped red pepper, 1 tbsp rinsed capers, 1 crushed garlic clove, 2 anchovy fillets, 1 tbsp black olives, 2 tbsp red wine vinegar and 3 tbsp extra virgin olive oil, and toss.

Avocado and lime toast Crush the flesh of 1 ripe avocado with a pinch of sea salt and a big squeeze of lime juice. Grill 2 thick slices of sourdough bread and brush with garlicky olive oil. Spread the avocado thickly on top and add plenty of black pepper. A brilliant breakfast for two.

Pain perdu au chocolat Make a batter by beating 2 eggs with 2 tbsp caster sugar, 100ml milk and 1 tsp cinnamon. Dip 4 thick slices of stale ciabatta bread in the batter and fry in 1 tbsp butter until golden and crisp. Drizzle with hot chocolate sauce or dip into mugs of hot chocolate.

peach bruschetta

dinner

Chinese roast pork

This isn't as scary as you think it's going to be. A good piece of belly pork is the easiest roast in the world, giving you tender meat topped with lots of crisp crackling. Serve sliced with steamed rice and Chinese greens, or cut into fingers to dip into hoisin sauce as a starter.

Wash and dry the belly pork, and score the skin at 1 cm intervals (for easy slicing later). Combine the salt and five spice powder and rub it all over the skin and meat. Set aside in the fridge for at least 2 hours.

Heat the oven to 230°C/Gas 8. Line a roasting tray with foil and place the pork on a rack set above the foil. Bake for 20 minutes.

SERVES 4

1 kg piece fresh belly pork
1 tbsp salt
3 tsp Chinese five spice powder
4 tbsp hoisin sauce

Lower the oven setting to 200°C/Gas 6 and bake for a further 45 minutes or until the skin crackles and crisps. If it doesn't totally crisp, finish the pork under the grill, being careful not to let it blister too much.

Remove the pork from the oven, and cut out any bones from the base. Cut the pork into thick slices, and then into thick fingers if you like. Serve warm, with hoisin sauce for dipping.

Pork chop with capers

A caper is a frisky leap or a dance. It's also the unopened flower bud of *Capparis spinosa*, a straggly, unkempt Mediterranean shrub. When cured, each little bud has the same sort of frisky effect in the mouth, especially in this lemony parsley dressing. Serve with a rocket salad and potatoes or a pumpkin mash.

To cook the pork chops, heat the olive oil in a non-stick frying pan. Lightly dust the chops in the flour, seasoned with salt, pepper and paprika; shake off any excess. Cook on one side over a moderate heat for around 8 minutes. Turn and cook on the other side for 5 minutes or until tender.

To make the dressing, pick the leaves from the parsley stems. Halve the tomato, squeeze out the seeds and juice, and finely chop the flesh. Mix the chopped tomato with the capers, parsley leaves, olive oil and lemon juice. Season with sea salt and pepper, and stir well.

Season the pork chops and place on warmed serving plates. Use a slotted spoon to spoon the dressing on and around each pork chop. Top with caper berries.

SERVES 4
4 large pork rib chops
2 tbsp olive oil
2 tbsp plain flour
½ tsp sea salt
½ tsp freshly ground black pepper
½ tsp smoked paprika or cayenne pepper
8 caper berries

Dressing:
good handful of flat-leaf parsley
1 ripe red tomato
1 tbsp capers, rinsed
3 tbsp extra virgin olive oil
1 tbsp lemon juice

Ham and mushroom pie

A nice big pie all to myself is my idea of comfort food, especially when frozen puff pastry makes it so simple.

Heat the oven to 200°C/Gas 6. Strip the thyme leaves from their stems. Heat the olive oil in a fry pan and gently cook the onion, garlic and thyme for 5 minutes. Slice the mushrooms, add to the pan and cook for 10 minutes until soft.

Shred the cooked ham or chicken, discarding any bones or skin. Off the heat, add to the mushroom mixture with the cooked peas. Season well with salt and pepper.

To make the sauce, melt the butter in a small saucepan, add the flour and cook, stirring, over a gentle heat for 3 minutes. Add a few spoonfuls of chicken stock and stir well, then add the remaining stock and bring to the boil, stirring constantly as the sauce thickens.

Add the cream, Worcestershire sauce, mustard, nutmeg and cayenne, and simmer gently for a couple of minutes, stirring. Add salt and pepper to taste, then strain the sauce over the filling and toss well.

Divide the filling between four individual pie dishes. Cover the tops with pastry, trimming to fit. Brush with beaten egg and bake for 30 minutes until puffy and golden.

MAKES 4
6 thyme sprigs
1 tbsp olive oil
1 onion, finely chopped
2 garlic cloves, smashed
500g button mushrooms
450g cooked ham or chicken
200g podded fresh or frozen peas, cooked
sea salt
freshly ground black pepper
500g packet ready-rolled frozen puff pastry, thawed
1 free-range egg, beaten

Sauce:
1 tbsp butter
1 tbsp flour
250ml chicken stock
2 tbsp cream
1 tbsp Worcestershire sauce
1 tsp Dijon mustard
½ tsp ground nutmeg
½ tsp cayenne pepper

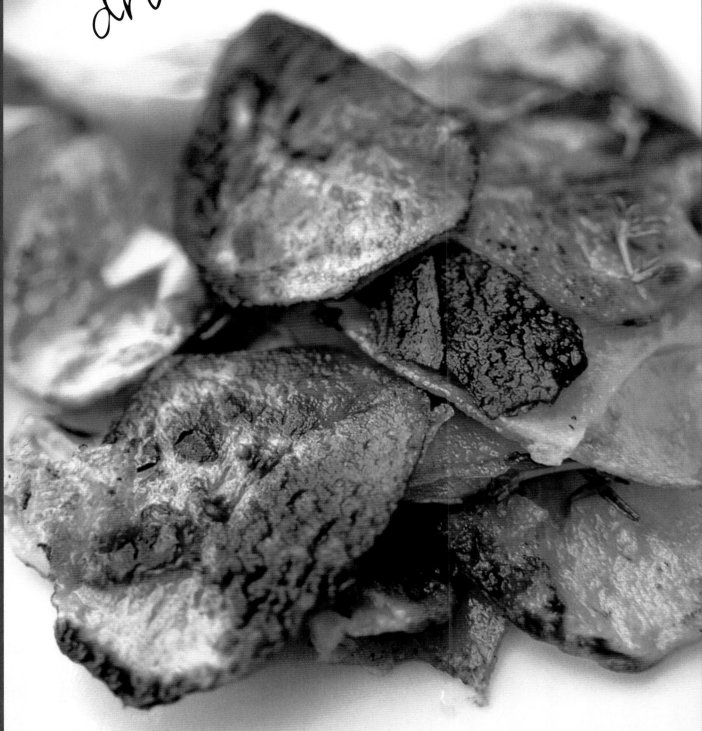

drunken potatoes

Lamb with tomatoes and olives

I grew up with the time-honoured roast lamb every Sunday, followed by variations on a theme of lamb most evenings during the week. You'd think I'd be over it, but instead I love cooking lamb at home, and ordering lamb when eating out. This is typical of the sort of thing I do at home when I'm pushed for time.

Place the lamb steaks between two sheets of cling film or greaseproof paper and bash them flat with a meat mallet or rolling pin. Place in a shallow dish and toss in the olive oil, garlic and rosemary sprigs.

SERVES 4

4 lamb steaks, around 180g
  each, or 2 lamb loin fillets
  (cut in two)
2 tbsp extra virgin olive oil
2 garlic cloves, smashed
2 rosemary sprigs
sea salt
freshly ground black pepper
200g cherry tomatoes
100g small black olives
  (eg Niçoise or Ligurian)

Heat a non-stick fry pan. When it is very hot, add the lamb (saving the marinade) and sear very quickly for a minute or two on each side, turning once. Remove the lamb to a plate while still pink inside, season with sea salt and pepper, and let it rest for a minute or two while you do the tomatoes.

Tip the reserved marinade into the pan, and add the cherry tomatoes and olives. Warm through until the tomatoes start to soften and burst.

Slice the lamb and arrange on warm plates. Tip the tomatoes and olives over the lamb and serve.

Drunken potatoes

This is my favourite new way of roasting potatoes because they absorb the flavour of the white wine they're cooked in, then turn crisp at the edges. For all those who loved the crash hot potatoes that appeared in Simple Food, you owe it to yourself to move on. Serve with grilled or pan-fried meat, poultry or fish, such as lamb with tomatoes (left), salt and pepper steak (page 80), jump-in-the-pan chicken (page 85), or cod in prosciutto (page 90).

Heat the oven to 200°C / Gas 6. Peel the potatoes and finely slice crosswise. Toss the potato slices in a bowl with the olive oil, sea salt and pepper. Lightly oil a baking tray (or deep-rimmed baking sheet) and scatter the potatoes loosely over the base. Pour over the white wine and scatter with the thyme.

Bake for 30 minutes, during which time the wine will boil and bubble away, and the potatoes will crisp to a beautiful golden crunch. Keep an eye on them during the last few minutes after the wine has evaporated, as they can over-crisp. The slices in the corners might get scorched, but it's worth the sacrifice.

Use a fish slice to lift the potatoes out of the pan, and serve hot.

SERVES 4
3 large, long potatoes,
around 750 g
2 tbsp extra virgin olive oil
sea salt
freshly ground black pepper
250 ml dry white wine
1 tbsp thyme sprigs

Salt and pepper steak

One of the tricks of good simple cooking is to upgrade your salt and pepper. I love soft-flaked Maldon sea salt, and buy fresh-tasting vine-ripened peppercorns from India. Sea salt is added to this pepper-crusted steak after cooking, not before, as it would draw out the juices from the meat. Serve with wilted spinach and potatoes.

Crush the peppercorns, then place in a fine sieve and shake to discard any fine dust. Tip the pepper onto a flat plate and press one side of each steak only into the mixture.

Heat the olive oil in a heavy non-stick frying pan. When hot, add the steaks, pepper-side down, and cook for 3 minutes over a moderate heat, without moving them. Turn once and cook for 2 to 3 minutes, depending on thickness. Transfer the steaks to warm plates.

Add the butter to the pan and melt. Add the brandy (carefully as it might flame), stirring well. Add the cream, mustard and a pinch of salt, stirring briskly as it bubbles. Pour into a warm jug. Scatter extra sea salt on the steaks and serve with the mustard sauce.

SERVES 2

1 tbsp black peppercorns

2 good rump or sirloin steaks, 200g each

1 tbsp olive oil

2 tbsp butter

1 tbsp brandy or Cognac

80ml double cream

2 tsp Dijon mustard

sea salt (eg Maldon)

Korean beef in lettuce

Tender beef is marinated in soy, garlic, ginger, spring onions and sesame oil, then flash-fried – so quickly that you need everyone waiting at the table before you begin.

Slice the beef thinly, against the grain. For the marinade, finely slice the spring onions and mix with the other ingredients; stir to dissolve the sugar. Add the beef, turn to coat and marinate for an hour or so.

Wash and dry the lettuce leaves; chill. For the soy chilli sauce, mix the sauces together in a bowl and set aside. Cook the jasmine rice until tender; keep warm.

Heat a heavy fry pan. When hot, sear the beef over high heat for 1 to 2 minutes, leaving it still pink in the middle. Scatter with sesame seeds and serve on warm plates, with hot rice and chilled lettuce.

Spoon a little jasmine rice onto a lettuce leaf, add a slice or two of spicy beef and a little soy chilli sauce, wrap the lettuce leaf around the filling and eat in the hands.

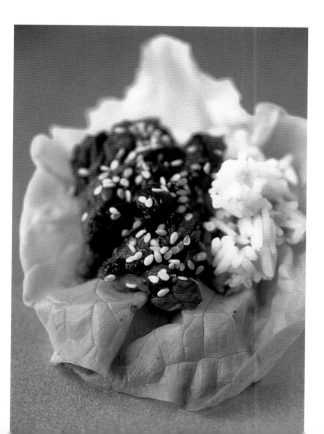

SERVES 4

2 sirloin steaks, 2.5 cm thick and around 250 g each
8 soft lettuce leaves (eg round, butter, oak leaf)
200 g jasmine rice
1 tbsp sesame seeds

Marinade:
2 spring onions
2 garlic cloves, crushed
5 cm knob of fresh root ginger, grated
1 tbsp sesame oil
2 tbsp rice wine or dry sherry
3 tbsp soy sauce
1 tbsp sweet chilli sauce or chilli bean sauce
1/2 tsp ground black pepper
1 tbsp sugar

Soy chilli sauce:
2 tbsp soy sauce
2 tbsp sweet chilli sauce or chilli bean sauce

Jump-in-the-pan chicken

This is an action dish, a simple sauté in the pan that creates its own creamy lemon and caper sauce for chicken. It's a terrific idea when you bring home the usual chicken breast and want to do something really fast. The trick is to keep the pan moving, jiggling it on the heat to make the chicken jump. Serve with rice, noodles or mash, or just a green salad.

Place each chicken breast between two sheets of cling film or greaseproof paper and bash flat with a meat mallet or rolling pin, and I mean as thin as a coin – almost breaking up.

Tear the chicken into little rags with your fingers, and toss lightly in the flour, seasoned with salt and pepper.

Heat the olive oil and butter in a large, heavy-based frying pan. When hot, add the chicken, scattering the pieces so they don't clump together. Instead of stirring, move the pan on the heat and flip the chicken pieces until lightly golden, so they jump in the pan.

Add the garlic, bay leaves, capers, sea salt and pepper. Remove the pan from the heat, add the wine, and return to a high heat. Let the wine bubble away, again jiggling the pan like crazy.

When there is only a little wine left, add the lemon juice and parsley leaves, and jiggle the pan until the sauce comes together and looks creamy. Serve immediately.

SERVES 4
3 skinless chicken breasts, around 150g each
2 tbsp plain flour
sea salt
freshly ground black pepper
2 tbsp olive oil
1 tbsp butter
1 garlic clove, crushed
4 bay leaves
2 tbsp capers, well rinsed
125ml dry white wine
1 tbsp lemon juice
2 tbsp flat-leaf parsley

Chicken and chickpea stew

A very satisfying chicken stew that takes some of the typical ingredients and flavours of Spain – sherry, paprika, chorizo sausages – and turns them into a lively, spicy winter meal you can have on the table within an hour of walking in the door.

Peel the carrots and potatoes and cut into bite-sized pieces. Dust the chicken lightly with flour, seasoned with salt and pepper. Heat 2 tbsp olive oil in a heavy fry pan and brown the chicken pieces.

Add the garlic, carrots, potatoes, paprika, bay leaves, salt and pepper. Add the sherry and water and bring to the boil, then simmer, covered, for about 20 minutes. Add the chickpeas, and cook for another 10 minutes or until the chicken is tender.

Thickly slice the chorizo and pan-fry in the remaining olive oil until sizzling. Add to the stew, scatter with parsley and serve.

SERVES 4

300 g carrots

500 g potatoes

8 chicken pieces (eg leg, thigh, breast)

1 tbsp plain flour

sea salt

freshly ground black pepper

3 tbsp olive oil

2 garlic cloves, smashed

1 tsp paprika

2 bay leaves

100 ml dry sherry

250 ml water

400 g canned chickpeas, rinsed

2 chorizo sausages, mild or hot

2 tbsp flat-leaf parsley

cod in prosciutto

Cod in prosciutto

Any firm white-fleshed fish can be cooked in this way. The outer covering of prosciutto or streaky bacon protects the fish and gives a good crisp texture. Simple, really. Serve with shredded cabbage and plenty of mash.

Trim the cod fillets into neat squares, season well and wrap in the prosciutto or bacon. Heat the oil in a fry pan and cook the fish on both sides until the prosciutto is lightly browned and the fish is cooked through, about 4 minutes each side, depending on thickness.

Remove the outer cabbage leaves, cut out any core and finely shred the leaves. Cook in simmering salted water for 5 minutes – the cabbage should have a soft crunch but still retain a bright colour. Drain well, return to the dry pan and toss with the butter or olive oil, vinegar, sugar, fennel or caraway seeds, sea salt and pepper.

Spoon the cabbage onto four warmed dinner plates, place the pan-fried fish on top and scatter with the thyme or parsley.

SERVES 4

4 cod fillets, around 180 g each
sea salt
freshly ground black pepper
4 wide or 8 thin slices
   prosciutto, or rindless
   streaky bacon
1 tbsp olive oil
½ Savoy cabbage, around 500g
2 tbsp butter or olive oil
1 tbsp red wine vinegar
1 tsp caster sugar
1 tsp fennel or caraway seeds
few thyme sprigs or parsley
   leaves

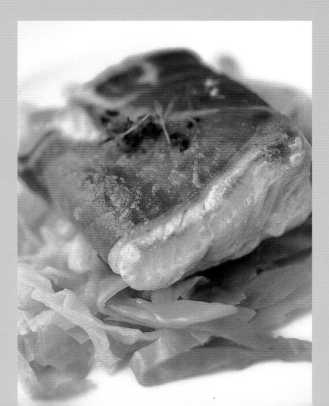

Insalata di mare

I love the Italian way with a seafood salad – all relaxed, sunny and easy – using good-flavoured olive oil and simple herbs. Chickpeas aren't usually served with seafood, but I can't for the life of me think why not.

Scrub the mussels and pull out the beards, discarding any that don't close when sharply tapped. Rinse the squid well and cut the tubes into 4 cm pieces. Score the insides lightly to help them curl.

Heat the olive oil, wine, peppercorns, garlic and parsley stems in a heavy lidded pan. Add the mussels, cover tightly and turn up the heat. Shake the pan after a minute or two, and take out any that have opened. Repeat twice, discarding any that don't open at all.

Strain the broth and return to the pan. Add the chickpeas and cook for 5 minutes. Add the squid and simmer for 1 minute or until just tender. Remove the squid and chickpeas with a slotted spoon and gently toss with the mussels, lemon juice, extra virgin olive oil, pepper and parsley. Add a spoonful or two of the seafood broth and serve warm or at room temperature, with lemon wedges.

SERVES 4
1 kg fresh mussels or clams
500 g cleaned small squid
(calamari)
2 tbsp olive oil
200 ml white wine
6 black peppercorns
2 garlic cloves, smashed
4 parsley stems
400 g canned chickpeas,
drained and rinsed
2 tbsp lemon juice
2 tbsp extra virgin olive oil
freshly ground black pepper
1 tbsp flat-leaf parsley
1 lemon, quartered

Goat cheese cannelloni

Rolling sheets of instant lasagne around a creamy cheese filling is a lot easier than stuffing cannelloni pasta tubes.

Heat the oven to 180°C / Gas 4. Bring a pot of salted water to the boil. Add the lasagne sheets, one at a time, and cook at a rolling boil until pliable, around 6 minutes. Drain and lay on a dry tea towel.

To make the filling, mash the ricotta, goat cheese, parsley, chives, salt, pepper and nutmeg together in a bowl.

Lay one sheet of lasagne on a board, spoon some of the mixture across the middle and roll into a cylinder. Place in a lightly greased baking dish. Repeat with the remaining lasagne and filling, laying the filled cannelloni side by side in the dish.

To make the sauce, whiz the tomatoes and their juice with the olive oil, sugar, and salt and pepper in a blender. Add the chopped herbs.

Pour the sauce over the cannelloni to cover completely. Scatter with parmesan and thyme, and bake for 30 minutes until bubbling hot.

SERVES 4
8 dried lasagne sheets
350g fresh ricotta cheese
100g soft, fresh goat cheese
2 tbsp finely chopped parsley
2 tsp finely snipped chives
$\frac{1}{2}$ tsp salt
$\frac{1}{2}$ tsp freshly ground black pepper
$\frac{1}{2}$ tsp ground nutmeg
2 tbsp finely grated parmesan
10 thyme sprigs

Sauce:
400g canned chopped tomatoes
1 tbsp olive oil
1 tsp sugar
1 tbsp chopped parsley
1 tbsp chopped thyme leaves

vegetables

Cabbage with cumin

How to turn a cabbage hater into a cabbage lover: buy the smallest, brightest, crispest and heaviest cabbage you can find, preferably the crinkly-leafed Savoy, cook it quickly and serve in a vinaigrette with cumin seeds.

Bring a large pan of water to the boil. Trim the base of the cabbage, but don't cut out the entire core as this will hold the wedges together. Cut the cabbage in half from top to bottom and then cut each half into three equal wedges. Discard the outer leaves that aren't up to scratch.

Add the salt to the boiling water and cook the cabbage wedges for 5 to 10 minutes or until they start to soften. Drain them well, upside down in a colander.

SERVES 4 TO 6

1 small, tight Savoy cabbage, around 1 kg

1/2 tsp salt

1 tbsp olive oil

1 tbsp white wine vinegar

1 tsp caster sugar

sea salt

freshly ground black pepper

2 tsp cumin or caraway seeds

Whisk the olive oil, wine vinegar, sugar, sea salt and pepper together in a bowl to make a vinaigrette. Arrange the cabbages on a serving platter and spoon over the vinaigrette. Scatter with cumin or caraway seeds and serve.

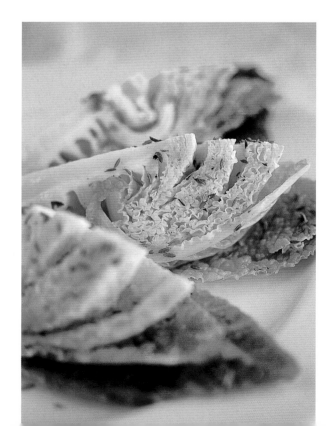

Pumpkin with raclette

Naturally sweet vegetables, such as pumpkin and butternut squash, are fantastic teamed with cheese. Raclette, fontina, and taleggio are all good melting cheeses, or use fresh mozzarella. Serve with a simple roast or a leafy green vegetable.

Heat the oven to 200°C / Gas 6. Cut the pumpkin or squash roughly into 2.5 cm cubes, cutting off any skin and discarding the seeds.

Steam the pumpkin cubes over fast boiling water for 20 minutes until tender, then drain and pile into a heatproof bowl or gratin dish. (If you don't have a steamer, put the cubes in a baking tray, add a dash of water, cover with foil and bake for 30 minutes or until tender.)

Cut the cheese into thin slices. Bake the pumpkin for 10 minutes or so, to help dry out the rather watery flesh, then top with the slices of cheese and bake for another minute or two until melted. Scatter with sea salt, pepper, oregano, sage and thyme, and serve.

SERVES 4
1 kg pumpkin or butternut squash
150 g raclette or other melting cheese
sea salt
freshly ground black pepper
few oregano sprigs
1 tbsp sage leaves
few thyme sprigs

beets and greens

Green veg frittata

A frittata is an Italian-style omelette that makes a simple lunch or supper. Use Swiss chard (silverbeet), ruby or rainbow chard, cavolo nero (black cabbage) or even green vegetables such as leeks, asparagus, peas and fine green beans.

Cut the stems from the Swiss chard and roughly chop. Cook in a large pot of simmering salted water for 10 minutes. Wash the leaves well, roughly chop, and add to the pot. Cook for 3 or 4 minutes until wilted. Drain well and cool, then squeeze out any excess water.

Beat the eggs, yolks, cream, cheese, salt, pepper and nutmeg in a bowl. Heat the butter and oil in a non-stick fry pan, then pour in the eggs. Scatter in the greens, jiggling them so they settle into the egg.

Cook over a moderate heat until the eggs have set on the bottom and are lightly golden. Heat the grill, protect the fry pan handle with foil and grill the frittata for a few minutes until lightly golden and just set in the middle. If it's still runny, cover the pan and place over a moderate heat for a minute or two. Cut into big wedges and serve.

SERVES 4 TO 6

1 kg Swiss chard (silverbeet)

6 free-range eggs, plus
   2 extra egg yolks

100 ml single cream

80 g freshly grated parmesan
   or gruyère

sea salt

freshly ground black pepper

$\frac{1}{2}$ tsp freshly grated nutmeg

1 tsp butter

2 tsp olive oil

Beets and greens

Buying baby beetroot without its ruby red stems and small bright green leaves is like buying asparagus without the tips. If the tops have already been guillotined, serve the beets on wilted spinach leaves or Swiss chard (silverbeet).

Cut the baby beetroot from their stems and cook unpeeled in simmering salted water for around 45 minutes until tender. Drain and cool, then rub off the skin with your fingers. Rinse well, toss the beets in 1 tbsp of the extra virgin olive oil and set aside.

Wash the leafy stems, and discard the thickest parts of the stems. Roughly chop the leaves and stems, keeping them separate.

Cook the stems in boiling salted water for 2 minutes, then add the leaves and cover. Simmer for 3 minutes until the leaves have wilted and the stems are tender. Drain well, and toss with the remaining extra virgin olive oil, lemon juice, sea salt and pepper.

Arrange on a large platter and tumble the baby beets on top. Serve warm or at room temperature with lemon wedges, as a side dish. Or serve as part of a meal of shared plates, perhaps with marinated feta, grilled lamb, and a tomato and cucumber salad.

SERVES 4
12 baby beetroot, with leaves
½ tsp salt
3 tbsp extra virgin olive oil
1 tbsp lemon juice
sea salt
freshly ground black pepper
1 lemon, quartered

Caponata

This is essentially a sweet and sour vegetable stew that began in the caupona, a type of osteria or tavern in southern Italy, which served cooked vegetables. Local sailors bought the vegetables while in port, then ate them flavoured with vinegar and sugar when at sea. Serve with lightly warmed pitta bread or flat bread.

Cut the aubergine into thick slices, then cut each slice into roughly 1cm cubes. Heat 2 tbsp olive oil in a fry pan and fry the aubergine briskly, tossing well, until golden and half cooked. Remove with a slotted spoon and set aside.

Add the remaining olive oil to the fry pan. When hot, add the onion and cook for 5 minutes until soft.

In the meantime, cut the tomatoes in half and squeeze out the seeds. Roughly chop the tomato flesh and add to the pan with the aubergine, celery, bay leaf, olives, salt and pepper. Cook for another 10 minutes.

Dissolve the sugar in the wine vinegar and add to the pan along with the capers. Cook for another 10 minutes until the aubergine is soft and there is no longer a sharp taste of vinegar.

Lightly toast the pine nuts in a hot, dry pan. Lightly warm the bread in a moderate oven or in a hot, dry pan for 2 minutes. Scatter the pine nuts over the vegetables, drizzle with olive oil and serve at room temperature, with a pile of warm bread.

SERVES 4 TO 6
2 medium aubergines
(eggplant)
3 tbsp olive oil
1 onion, finely chopped
4 medium tomatoes
2 celery sticks, finely sliced
1 bay leaf
3 tbsp green olives, stoned
sea salt
freshly ground black pepper
1 tbsp sugar
2 tbsp red wine vinegar
1 tbsp capers, rinsed
2 tbsp pine nuts

To serve:
6–8 flat or pitta breads
extra virgin olive oil

Mallorcan tumbet

I came across these layered baked vegetables in Mallorca, where they are cooked in a terracotta 'cassola'. I'm all for using canned tomatoes to make a sauce, especially in winter.

To make the sauce, combine the tomatoes, oregano, garlic and olive oil with sea salt and pepper in a saucepan, and simmer, covered, for 20 minutes. Heat the oven to 180°C/Gas 4.

Peel and finely slice the potatoes. Finely slice the aubergines. Cut the peppers into long thin fingers, discarding core and seeds. Heat 2 tbsp olive oil in a fry pan and gently fry the potato slices in batches, until golden on both sides. Layer in a 1 litre baking dish and season.

Add the remaining olive oil to the pan and fry the aubergine until well browned. Arrange over the potatoes and season. Fry the red peppers, then layer on top of the aubergines.

Spoon the tomato sauce over the top of the vegetables and bake for 20 minutes until bubbling hot. Serve warm or at room temperature, as a starter or side dish, or as a main course for two.

SERVES 4

400g all-purpose potatoes

400g aubergines (eggplant)

2 sweet red peppers

3 tbsp olive oil

sea salt

freshly ground black pepper

Sauce:

400g canned tomatoes, chopped

3 oregano sprigs, or 1 tsp dried oregano

3 garlic cloves, finely sliced

2 tbsp olive oil

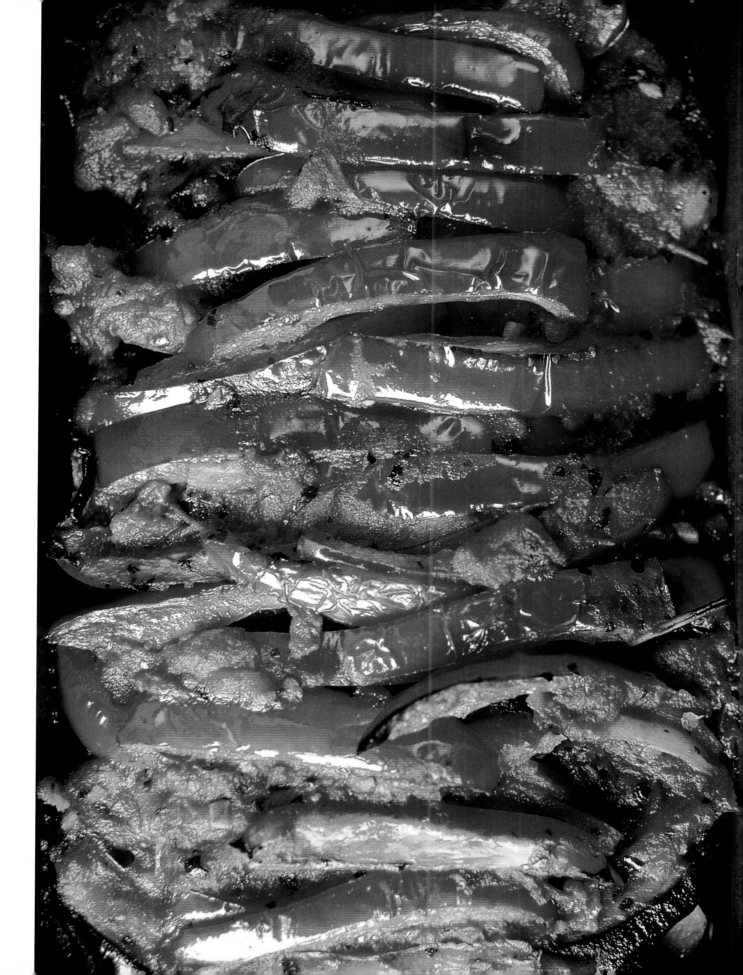

Peas and bacon

Peas should be revered as they were in the seventeenth century, when the sophisticated Madame de Maintenon from the French court of Louis XIV wrote of the royal courtiers' obsession with peas as 'both a fashion and a madness'.

Cook the peas in simmering salted water until just tender. Drain, refresh with cold water, drain well and set aside. (You can do this ahead of time.)

SERVES 4

600g podded fresh or
**   frozen peas**
salt
6 shallots, or 1 small red onion
100g thick rindless bacon
**   rashers**
2 tbsp butter
100ml chicken stock or dry
**   white wine**
1 tsp caster sugar
sea salt
freshly ground black pepper

Peel and slice the shallots, and finely chop the bacon. Heat half the butter in a pan and gently cook the shallots and bacon for 5 minutes. Add the stock or wine and bring to the boil, then reduce to a simmer.

Add the peas, sugar, sea salt, plenty of black pepper and the remaining butter. Gently heat through and simmer until the liquid is reduced to a couple of tablespoonfuls, then serve.

paper bag veggies

Paper bag veggies

A splendid vegetarian dinner is in the bag with these baked paper 'purses' of steamy spiced vegetables, served with a bowl of garlicky herbed crème fraîche. Make sure you have enough greaseproof or baking paper to make the bags.

Heat the oven to 200°C/Gas 6. Trim the leeks and cut into 1 cm slices. Peel the potatoes, sweet potato and parsnips, and cut into chunky bite-sized pieces. Cut the courgettes and red pepper into similar pieces, discarding the pepper core and seeds.

In a large bowl, mix the olive oil with the saffron, thyme, rosemary, sea salt and pepper. Add the vegetables and toss well.

Cut four rounds of greaseproof paper, 36 cm in diameter. Divide the vegetables between them, scatter with fennel seeds and bring the paper up evenly around each pile of vegetables, pursing it together at the top and tying securely with string.

Place the bags on a baking sheet and bake for 30 to 40 minutes or until an inserted skewer meets with no resistance. Meanwhile, beat the garlic and parsley into the crème fraîche and set aside.

To serve, snip the paper parcels open below the string, and serve in or out of the paper, with the herbed crème fraîche.

SERVES 4

2 leeks

4 smallish potatoes

1 medium sweet potato

2 medium parsnips

2 medium courgettes

1 sweet red pepper

4 tbsp extra virgin olive oil

1/2 tsp powdered saffron

4 thyme sprigs

4 rosemary sprigs

sea salt

freshly ground black pepper

1 tbsp fennel seeds

To serve:

2 garlic cloves, crushed

2 tbsp finely chopped parsley

200g crème fraîche

Black olive roast veg

I always keep a jar of pesto and a jar of olive tapenade in the fridge door next to the Campari and soda. They're great instant flavour hits if you don't want to do much more than grill some sourdough bread or cook some pasta for dinner.

Heat the oven to 200°C / Gas 6. Cut the pumpkin into thinnish wedges, trim off the skin, and discard any seeds. Peel the potatoes and cut in half. Wash the carrots, trim the tops neatly, and peel. Peel the parsnips and cut lengthwise into quarters.

Combine the tapenade with the olive oil and pepper in a big bowl. Add the vegetables, rosemary and garlic cloves and toss until well coated. Tip into a baking tray and bake for 45 minutes to 1 hour, until the vegetables are tender and nicely browned.

Pile the roast vegetables onto warm plates and tuck in a few fresh rosemary sprigs. Top with a spoonful of olive tapenade, thinned with a little olive oil.

SERVES 4
500 g pumpkin
500 g smallish potatoes
2 bunches baby carrots
4 parsnips
2 tbsp black olive tapenade
2 tbsp extra virgin olive oil
1/2 tsp freshly ground black pepper
4 rosemary sprigs
4 garlic cloves (unpeeled)

To serve:
rosemary sprigs
extra black olive tapenade
a little extra virgin olive oil

Vegetable curry

For me, an Indian vegetable curry should be warmly spiced, rather than chilli-hot, with meltingly soft vegetables, and a sauce that calls for a huge mound of rice. Done.

Finely slice the onion. Peel and roughly chop the potatoes. Peel and quarter the carrot and parsnips lengthwise. Cut the aubergine, courgette and red pepper into chunks, discarding the pepper core and seeds.

Heat the oil in a heavy-based frying pan and add the mustard seeds and fenugreek. When the seeds start to pop, add the cumin, turmeric, ginger and paprika, stirring. Add the onion and cook for 5 minutes until softened.

Add the potatoes and fry lightly, then add the carrot, parsnips, aubergine, courgette and red pepper, stirring. Add the water, tomato purée, salt, sugar, curry leaves and cinnamon stick, and bring to the boil.

Simmer, uncovered, for 30 to 40 minutes or until the vegetables are soft and the liquid is reduced to a sauce, stirring occasionally. Serve with plenty of rice.

SERVES 4

1 onion, peeled

500g all-purpose potatoes

1 carrot, peeled

2 parsnips, peeled

1 aubergine (eggplant)

1 courgette (zucchini)

1 sweet red pepper

2 tbsp vegetable oil

2 tsp mustard seeds

½ tsp fenugreek seeds

1 tsp ground cumin

1 tsp ground turmeric

1 tsp ground ginger

½ tsp paprika

1 litre water or stock

1 tbsp tomato purée (paste)

1 tsp salt

1 tsp soft brown sugar

few curry leaves

1 cinnamon stick

potato

Potato and borlotti mash Cook 1 kg potatoes with 2 peeled garlic cloves until tender, adding 400g drained, canned borlotti beans for the last minute. Drain and return to the pan. Add 2 tbsp extra virgin olive oil, 1 tbsp chopped parsley, sea salt and pepper. Mash, keeping it chunky.

Greek red potatoes Par-boil 1 kg peeled, quartered waxy potatoes for 10 minutes; drain. Toss with 2 tbsp tomato purée, 2 tbsp extra virgin olive oil, 2 tbsp water, salt and pepper. Bake on a foil-lined tray at 200°C/Gas 6 for 20 minutes until tender. Serve with roast lamb or grilled fish.

Floury or waxy? Use floury potatoes such as King Edward, Maris Piper, pink-skinned Desirée and Romano for mashing, roasting and frying. Choose waxy potatoes – Charlotte, La Ratte, Jersey Royal, Kipfler, Belle de Fontenay and Pink Fir Apple – for simple boiled potatoes and salads.

Warm saffron potato salad Whisk 2 tbsp extra virgin olive oil with 1 tbsp mayonnaise, 1 tbsp lemon juice, 1 tsp tomato purée, 1 tsp Dijon mustard, $1/2$ tsp powdered saffron, $1/2$ tsp paprika, sea salt and pepper. Thickly slice 1 kg boiled potatoes. Toss in the dressing while still warm.

Potato, tuna and olive salad Drain and flake 400g canned tuna in oil. Whisk 3 tbsp extra virgin olive oil, 3 tbsp white wine and 2 tbsp lemon juice with salt and pepper. Thickly slice 600g boiled waxy potatoes and toss in the dressing. Add the tuna and 20 black olives. Serve with rocket.

Is it cooked? When you boil potatoes, spear one with a thin bamboo skewer so the stick pokes up out of the water. To check if the potatoes are cooked, pick up the bamboo stick. If the potato clings to it, it's not yet cooked. If it slips off, it's perfect. Brilliant!

Goose fat potatoes Peel 3 medium waxy potatoes and cut into 2cm dice. Fry gently in 100g goose or duck fat with 2 garlic cloves for 20 minutes, tossing occasionally, then turn up the heat and cook until crisp and brown. Drain, toss with sea salt and pepper, and serve.

Belgian stoemp Cook 750g potatoes with 3 finely sliced leeks until tender. Drain and lightly mash with butter, salt, pepper and a little grated nutmeg. Serve with sausages, grilled fish or a thick slice of leg ham.

Herring and potato salad Dress 600g hot boiled potatoes with 2 tbsp olive oil, 2 tbsp white wine, 2 tbsp red wine vinegar and 1 tbsp Dijon mustard. Add a dollop of sour cream, 1 tbsp capers, lots of pepper, and a little finely sliced shallot. Drape 4 marinated herrings on top.

Choucroute for cheats Cook 1kg small peeled potatoes until tender. Heat 300g prepared sauerkraut in a pan with 1 tsp caraway seeds and 100ml white wine. Simmer 4 frankfurters and 4 weisswurst for 5 minutes, drain and serve on the sauerkraut and potatoes, with Dijon mustard.

Smoked salmon potato Prick 4 large baking potatoes, coat lightly in olive oil and roll in a little sea salt and cracked black pepper. Bake at 200°C/Gas 6 for $1^1/_2$ hours until soft. Cut open, top with crème fraîche, smoked salmon, horseradish sauce and chives.

Six more baked potato toppings Bake 4 large potatoes (as above), and top with: poached egg and crisped bacon; caramelised onions; pan-fried mushrooms and chives; pan-fried chicken livers; wilted rocket and gorgonzola; or roasted red peppers tossed with capers and anchovies.

goose fat potatoes

family

Spicy pork noodles

This is the Chinese equivalent of spaghetti Bolognese. Brown bean sauce is available from Asian food stores.

Mix the brown bean sauce, hoisin, soy sauce, water and sugar together in a bowl, stirring. Set aside.

Peel the cucumber, and pare lengthwise with a vegetable peeler into ribbons. Cut the ribbons into matchsticks and set aside.

Heat a wok or fry pan. When hot, add the oil and stir-fry most of the spring onions for 30 seconds. Add the pork and stir-fry for a few minutes until browned. Add the sauce mix and stir-fry for about 5 minutes until the water has evaporated, oil rises to the surface, and the pork smells sweet and spicy. Mix the cornflour with the water or rice wine, and add to the meat, stirring.

Place the noodles in a large heatproof bowl and cover with a kettleful of boiling water. Drain well and return to the bowl. Add the spicy pork sauce and toss well. Divide between four deep warmed bowls, scatter with cucumber and spring onions and serve with chopsticks.

SERVES 4

1 tbsp brown bean or chilli
   bean sauce

1 tbsp hoisin sauce

2 tbsp soy sauce

125 ml water

1 tsp soft brown sugar

1/2 cucumber

2 tbsp peanut oil

4 spring onions, finely chopped

500 g minced pork

1 tbsp cornflour

1 tbsp water or Chinese rice
   wine

500 g fresh oiled egg noodles
   (Hokkien)

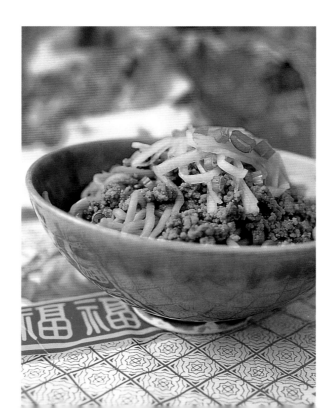

Long life noodles

Cantonese legend has it that the longer the noodle, the longer you will live. Or it could just be that noodles are good for you.

Put the dried mushrooms in a bowl, pour on the boiling water and soak for at least 30 minutes. Cut the white leek into 5cm lengths, halve lengthwise, then cut into very thin matchstick strips.

Lift the mushrooms from the water, discard the stems and slice the caps finely; set aside. Strain 100ml of the soaking water into a bowl and stir in the soy sauce, oyster sauce, sesame oil and sugar; set aside. Place the noodles in a large heatproof bowl and pour a kettleful of boiling water over the top, then drain well.

Heat the wok. When hot, add the oil and stir-fry the ginger and garlic for 1 minute. Add the leek and mushrooms, tossing well over a high heat. Add the sauce, bring to the boil and cook, stirring, for 1 minute.

Add the tofu and cook for 1 minute. Add the noodles, and cook for about 2 minutes, tossing, until they have absorbed most of the sauce. Scatter with spring onions and serve with chopsticks.

SERVES 4
6 dried Chinese mushrooms
200ml boiling water
1 leek, white part only
2 tbsp soy sauce
1 tbsp oyster sauce
1 tsp sesame oil
1 tsp sugar
450g fresh oiled egg noodles (Hokkien)
1 tbsp vegetable oil
1 tbsp grated fresh root ginger
2 garlic cloves, crushed
200g tofu, drained and cut into cubes
2 spring onions, finely sliced

burger with the lot

Burger with the lot

The hamburger is a legitimate and respectable meal of grilled meat and salad served with bread. It's just served vertically, instead of horizontally. The real key to a good burger is in the build, which is both an art and a science.

SERVES 4
Burgers:
2 slices white bread
100 ml milk
500 g prime minced beef
1 tbsp finely snipped chives
1 tbsp finely chopped parsley
sea salt
freshly ground black pepper
1 free-range egg, lightly
   beaten
4 slices bacon or pancetta
1 tbsp olive oil

To serve:
4 slices cheese (eg jarlsberg)
4 hamburger buns
4 tbsp tomato relish (see right)
8 lettuce leaves
2 tomatoes, thickly sliced
2 tbsp quality mayonnaise

To make the burgers, soak the bread in the milk, squeeze dry and chop finely. In a bowl, mix the minced beef with the bread, chives, parsley, salt and pepper. Add the egg, and mix to a mulch with your hands. Form into four thick bun-sized patties, cover and chill.

Grill or pan-fry the bacon or pancetta until crisp. Heat the olive oil in a heavy-based frying pan and cook the burgers for 3 minutes on each side until well browned. Top each with a cheese slice as it comes off the heat.

Split the buns, and lightly toast the insides only. Top the base bun in this order: tomato relish, lettuce leaves, cheese burger, bacon and a slice of tomato. Spread the mayonnaise on the inside lid and place on top.

Tomato relish

Combine 400 g canned chopped tomatoes, 2 tbsp olive oil, 1 finely chopped onion, 2 crushed garlic cloves, 2 tbsp wine vinegar and 1 tbsp sugar in a saucepan. Season and cook down until thick and pulpy, stirring occasionally.

Turkey burger

Go beyond the beef burger to the turkey or chicken burger, which is lighter and sweeter. If you find hamburger buns a bit soft and squishy, try lightly toasted English muffins. These are slightly smaller, so it is easier to shape your burger to them.

In a bowl, combine the minced meat, thyme or parsley, breadcrumbs, egg, and salt and pepper, and mix with your hands to a mulch. Form the mixture into four balls, then flatten into muffin-sized patties.

If grilling, brush the meat with the olive oil. If pan-frying, heat the oil in a heavy-based frying pan. Grill or fry the burgers on both sides until brown and sizzling. This should take around 5 minutes on each side, but check one before serving.

Split the muffins and lightly toast or grill the insides only. Top each muffin base with a lettuce leaf, cucumber slices and the burger, adding tomato and avocado slices if you like. Top with cranberry sauce and mayonnaise, and finally the bun lid.

SERVES 4
Burgers:
450g minced turkey or chicken
1 tbsp thyme leaves or chopped parsley
3 tbsp fresh or dried breadcrumbs
1 free-range egg, lightly beaten
sea salt
freshly ground black pepper
1 tbsp olive oil

To serve:
4 English muffins or hamburger buns
4 soft lettuce leaves
1/2 cucumber, peeled and sliced
2 tbsp cranberry sauce
2 tbsp quality mayonnaise

Extras:
2 tomatoes, sliced
1/2 avocado, sliced

chicken stir-fry

Chicken stir-fry

The three rules of the stir-fry are: keep it hot, keep it moving and keep it simple. Flip the food constantly in the wok, and it will stay bright and clear-tasting. It also pays to get everything ready and lined up in order, so nothing is forgotten. (Saves you from that old oops-forgot-to-add-the-chicken syndrome.)

Finely slice the chicken breasts and cut each slice in half. Mix 1 tbsp soy sauce, 1 tbsp rice wine and 1 tsp cornflour together in a bowl. Add the chicken and turn to coat well. Set aside to marinate.

Slice the mangetout lengthwise with the tip of a sharp knife – a bit of an effort but worth it for the effect. Finely slice the celery. Mix the remaining rice wine and cornflour together and set aside.

Heat the wok until hot. When hot, add the oil and stir-fry the garlic and ginger for 30 seconds. Add the chicken with its marinade, and toss well over a high heat for 2 minutes until coloured.

Add the mangetout, celery and bean sprouts, and toss over high heat for 2 minutes. Add the oyster sauce and remaining soy, and toss for 2 minutes. Add the cornflour mixture and bring to the boil, tossing.

Divide the stir-fry between four deep warmed bowls and serve with bowls of rice and chopsticks.

SERVES 4

2 chicken breast fillets

3 tbsp soy sauce

2 tbsp Chinese rice wine or
   dry sherry

2 tsp cornflour

200g mangetout (snow peas)

2 celery sticks

2 tbsp vegetable oil

1 garlic clove, squashed

1 slice fresh root ginger,
   shredded

200g bean sprouts, rinsed

2 tbsp oyster sauce

Chinese spiced beef

A simple, old-fashioned cut of meat cooks itself to tenderness in this classic Chinese braise. I serve it with the garlic, ginger and whole spices intact, but you can fish them out if you like.

Cut the beef into 2.5 cm cubes. Heat the oil in a flameproof casserole or heavy-based saucepan and brown the meat lightly, in batches. Return all meat to the pan and add cold water to cover. Bring to the boil, then immediately reduce to a simmer, skimming if necessary.

Stir in the rice wine, garlic, ginger, spring onions, soy sauce, sugar, star anise and cinnamon sticks. Simmer very gently, partly covered, for 2 hours. Meanwhile, soak the mushrooms in the hot water.

Cut the pumpkin into 2 cm cubes, discarding seeds and skin. Drain and halve the mushrooms, discarding stalks.

Add the pumpkin and mushrooms to the braise and cook uncovered, for another 30 minutes until the beef is tender. Serve in warm bowls, with lots of rice.

SERVES 4

1 kg beef brisket

2 tbsp vegetable oil

3 tbsp Chinese rice wine or dry sherry

2 garlic cloves, bruised

3 thick slices fresh root ginger

3 spring onions, finely chopped

125 ml soy sauce

3 tbsp soft brown sugar

4 star anise

4 cinnamon sticks

8 dried Chinese mushrooms

200 ml hot water

500 g pumpkin or butternut squash

Cavatappi with sausage

Cavatappi is my pasta of the moment, because its corkscrew curls catch and keep all the sauce. And this is my favourite sauce – spicy Italian pork sausage cooked in milk (a grand-motherly trick to make it sweet), and then in tomato. You can't get more comforting than that.

Slit open the sausages and remove the meat, discarding the skins. Finely slice the onion. Heat the olive oil and butter in a fry pan and cook the onion gently for 5 or 6 minutes until soft but not coloured.

Pinch the meat into the pan and fry, breaking it up with a wooden spoon, until it is cooked but not browned. Add the milk and simmer very gently, stirring, for 5 minutes until it is all absorbed.

Roughly chop the tomatoes and add them, with their juices, to the pan. Add the sugar, nutmeg, and salt and pepper, and simmer for 15 minutes, stirring occasionally.

In the meantime, cook the pasta in a large pot of boiling salted water until al dente, tender but still firm to the bite.

Add the cream to the sauce and stir, gently heating it through. Drain the pasta, toss well with the sauce and serve with plenty of grated parmesan.

SERVES 4
6 small, spicy Italian pork sausages, or 3 large ones
1 small onion, peeled
1 tbsp olive oil
1 tbsp butter
150 ml milk
400 g canned tomatoes
1 tsp sugar
pinch of freshly grated nutmeg
sea salt
freshly ground black pepper
400 g cavatappi, penne or other short tube pasta
2 tbsp cream (optional)
freshly grated parmesan

Beans and wilted rocket

I suspect I spend more on peppery, horseradishy rocket than I do on shoes. I wilt it into pasta, scatter it over risotto and stews, serve it with seafood grills, and generally munch my way through bowls of the stuff. This is a fast (rocket-fuelled) way to get lunch on the table.

Heat 2 tbsp olive oil in a saucepan. Add the garlic, tomatoes or passata, sugar, Worcestershire sauce and mustard, and cook gently for 10 minutes, stirring. Add the beans and parsley, and cook for a further 5 minutes, adding a little water if it gets too thick. Season with salt and pepper to taste.

Drop the rocket into a pot of simmering salted water for a few seconds until just wilted, then drain well, squeeze out excess water, and chop roughly. Toss in 1 tbsp olive oil, with sea salt and pepper.

Grill or toast four thick slices of sourdough bread. Top each slice with the wilted rocket, and spoon the hot beans over the top.

SERVES 6

3 tbsp extra virgin olive oil

2 garlic cloves, crushed

400 g canned tomatoes, chopped
   or 500 ml tomato passata
   (puréed tomatoes)

1 tbsp soft brown sugar

1 tbsp Worcestershire sauce

1 tsp Dijon mustard

800 g canned white beans
   (cannellini or white kidney
   beans), drained and rinsed

2 tbsp finely chopped parsley

sea salt

freshly ground black pepper

250 g rocket leaves

4 thick slices sourdough bread

terry's fried egg

Terry's fried egg roll

My football-mad husband has devised a number of different things to eat while watching sport on television. For this simple half-time lunch, he has even developed a brilliant technique for cooking the perfect fried egg.

Heat the olive oil in a non-stick pan. Break in the eggs, cover the pan with a lid and cook over a very gentle heat for 4 to 5 minutes, depending on the heat, until the whites have set and the yolks have glazed over but are still softly runny.

In the meantime, lightly warm the baguette in the oven for 2 minutes, or split in half and lightly grill the inside surfaces.

Halve the cherry tomatoes. Heat 1 tbsp olive oil in a non-stick fry pan. Add the tomatoes and cook for 2 minutes, until they soften.

Place the split baguettes on two warm plates and lightly butter if you like. Line each one with ham, place a fried egg on top and spoon the cherry tomatoes over. Scatter with salt and pepper and serve.

MAKES 2

Terry's fried eggs:

1 tsp olive oil

2 free-range eggs

To serve:

1 fresh baguette

4 cherry tomatoes

1 tbsp olive oil

butter to spread (optional)

2 thin slices good ham

sea salt

freshly ground black pepper

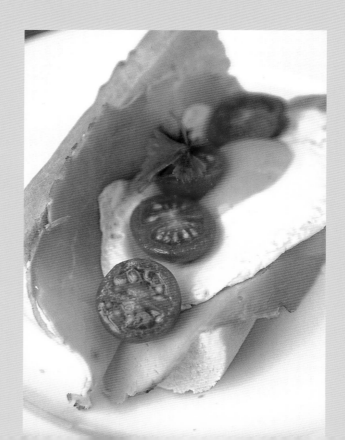

Chorizo and potatoes

Use mild or spicy chorizo sausages from the deli or butcher, and serve this lovely Spanish tapa dish with crusty bread and a glass of red.

Peel the potatoes and cut into roughly 1 cm dice. Cook in simmering salted water for 10 minutes, until half-cooked.

Slice the chorizo, and finely slice the onion and celery. Heat half the oil in a heavy-based fry pan and sear the chorizo on both sides until browned. Remove the chorizo, then add the remaining oil to the pan and cook the onion and celery for 5 minutes to soften.

Add the potatoes, garlic, sea salt, pepper, and half the paprika; toss well. Add the white wine, bay leaf and enough water to cover the potatoes. Cook, uncovered, over a medium heat for 10 minutes or until the potatoes are tender.

Return the chorizo to the pan and cook on a high heat for a further 5 minutes or until the liquid reduces to a sludgy sauce. Serve warm or at room temperature, scattered with the remaining paprika.

SERVES 4

500 g all-purpose potatoes

salt

2 chorizo sausages

1 onion, peeled

1 celery stick

2 tbsp olive oil

1 garlic clove, smashed

sea salt

freshly ground black pepper

1 tsp paprika

200 ml dry white wine

1 bay leaf

Stuffed peppers

It's time some of these old-fashioned ideas were brought back into circulation, because they work. Stuff a sweet pepper with meat and rice, and the juices will mingle as the stuffing virtually steams and the pepper cooks, so that the two are one.

Heat the oven to 200°C/Gas 6. Cut the tops off the peppers, retaining them to use as lids. Scoop out the seeds and cut away any major internal ribbing from the insides.

In a bowl, mix the minced meat with the egg, cooked rice, spring onions, half the paprika, parsley, sea salt and pepper, mulching it with your hands. Add half the tomatoes, mixing well.

Stuff the peppers with the mixture, piling it high. Stand the peppers in a lightly oiled baking tin and rub the skin with a little of the olive oil. Bake for 1 hour, or until tender, adding the lightly oiled pepper lids to the tin for the last 15 minutes.

To make the sauce, gently heat the rest of the chopped tomatoes with the remaining olive oil, paprika, sugar, salt and pepper.

To serve, place a whole stuffed pepper on each plate, spoon the tomato sauce on and around, and top with the lid.

SERVES 4
2 sweet red peppers
2 sweet yellow peppers
500g minced pork or chicken
1 free-range egg
150g cooked rice
4 spring onions, finely chopped
1 tsp paprika
1 tbsp finely chopped parsley
sea salt
freshly ground black pepper
400g canned chopped tomatoes
2 tbsp olive oil
1 tsp sugar

special

Scallop stack

Beautiful, big, hand-dived scallops may be expensive, but they are worth it. Avoid scallops that have been soaked in water, as these will stew rather than sear, spoiling the dish. To turn this elegant starter into a main course, serve with lemony couscous.

Rinse and dry the scallops. Cut a cross in the base of the tomatoes and dunk them into a pot of boiling water for 20 seconds. Remove and peel. Cut in half, discard the juices and seeds, then cut the flesh into small dice.

Whisk the extra virgin olive oil and lemon juice in a bowl, with sea salt and pepper. Add the diced tomatoes, preserved lemon and basil or parsley. Toss lightly and set aside.

SERVES 4

12 large sea scallops, cleaned

2 ripe red tomatoes

3 tbsp extra virgin olive oil

1 tbsp lemon juice, or more

sea salt

freshly ground black pepper

1 tbsp finely chopped
   preserved lemon

2 tbsp chopped basil or
   flat-leaf parsley

1 tbsp olive oil

Heat the olive oil in a heavy-based fry pan and sear the scallops on one side, without moving, for 2 minutes, until crusty. Turn and cook on the other side for less than a minute, or until hot in the middle but still moist. Season well with sea salt and pepper.

Stack three scallops on each plate and drizzle with the tomato and lemon vinaigrette to serve.

Thai seafood soup

'Dtom yam gung' is the most famous of all Thai soups, for its provocative balance of chilli, lime juice and fish sauce. Making the stock from the prawn heads gives that authentic touch of 'red oil' to the broth.

Peel and devein the prawns, saving the heads and shells. Heat the oil in a heavy-based fry pan, add the prawn heads and shells, and toss well over a fairly high heat, then crush with a potato masher to extract the juices. Add the boiling water and simmer for 10 minutes.

Finely slice the chilli and mushrooms. Strain the prawn stock through a sieve into a saucepan, discarding the heads and shells. Add the lemongrass, chilli, mushrooms and lime leaves, and simmer for 5 minutes. Add the prawns, sugar and fish sauce, and simmer for a couple of minutes until the prawns turn pink.

Remove from the heat, add the lime juice and half the coriander, and taste for the balance between hot, sweet and sour flavours. Serve in four deep soup bowls, scattered with the remaining coriander.

SERVES 4

8 to 12 medium raw prawns in shell
1 tbsp vegetable oil
1 litre boiling water
1 small red chilli
150g button mushrooms or straw mushrooms
2 lemongrass stalks, white part only, bashed
4 kaffir lime leaves
1 tbsp sugar
2 tbsp Thai fish sauce
3 tbsp lime juice, or more to taste
3 tbsp coriander leaves

Asparagus and pea soup

As with any green vegetable soup, I suggest whizzing a handful of fresh flat-leaf parsley into the finished soup just before serving, to intensify the freshness and the colour. And don't feel you have to stand a spear of asparagus in the soup as I did for the photograph here. All cooks have their own ways of amusing themselves, and this was mine.

Wash the asparagus, then bend the spears until they snap and discard the woody ends. Finely chop the asparagus, reserving the tips for serving.

Bring the chicken stock to the boil, add the asparagus and green peas and simmer for 15 minutes until soft. Add sea salt and pepper and taste.

Cool the soup a little, then purée in the blender or food processor in batches. Add the parsley leaves to the last batch, and whiz.

To serve, gently reheat the soup and the asparagus tips for about 5 minutes, then ladle into four warmed soup bowls. I don't think it needs cream, but you could add a spoonful or two when reheating if you're feeling creamy.

SERVES 6

1 kg thick asparagus

1.2 litres chicken stock

250 g podded fresh or frozen peas

sea salt

freshly ground black pepper

handful of flat-leaf parsley leaves

saffron cream mussels

Saffron cream mussels

A touch of saffron and curry powder in the creamy sauce makes these mussels irresistible. Cook the mussels lightly so they are plump, sweet and still full of their own juices.

Discard any broken mussels, and those that do not close when sharply tapped. Scrub the mussels well and pull out the little beards. Put the white wine, onion and garlic in a heavy lidded fry pan, bring to the boil and boil for 1 minute. Add the mussels, cover tightly and cook for 1 minute.

Shake the pan and remove any mussels that have opened, then repeat the process, keeping the opened mussels in a covered bowl. Discard any mussels that remain closed. Strain the cooking broth into a jug and set aside.

SERVES 4

1.5kg mussels

125ml dry white wine

1 small onion, finely chopped

1 garlic clove, finely chopped

1 tbsp butter

1 tbsp plain flour

100ml milk

1 egg yolk

1/2 tsp mild curry powder

1/2 tsp powdered saffron

1/2 tsp ground turmeric

100ml double cream or
   whipping cream

Melt the butter in a small saucepan, scatter on the flour and cook, stirring, for about 3 minutes. Gradually pour in the mussel broth, stirring constantly, then slowly pour in the milk, stirring.

Beat the egg yolk, curry powder, saffron, turmeric and cream together, then add to the sauce, stirring well; don't let it boil.

Remove the top shells of about half the mussels, and discard. Pile all the mussels into four warmed shallow bowls and pour the sauce over the top to serve.

Red mullet with laksa sauce

Singaporean laksa is usually a soup with noodles, but I've borrowed the rich, creamy sauce for a special dinner. Keep a jar of curry laksa paste on hand and it's made in 10 minutes. Do it again with salmon, bream, or even prawns, chicken or vegetables, and serve with rice or noodles.

Peel the cucumber and slice it as finely as you can. Salt the cucumber and set aside.

To make the sauce, heat the oil in a fry pan or wok. Add the curry laksa paste and fry for 3 or 4 minutes until fragrant. Add the chicken stock, salt and sugar and bring to the boil. Reduce to a simmer and add the coconut milk, stirring constantly. Simmer uncovered for 5 minutes until lightly creamy.

To cook the fish, heat the oil in a non-stick fry pan and cook the fillets, skin-side down, for 2 to 3 minutes, gently pressing them into the pan to help crisp the skin. Turn and cook the other side for 1 minute. Season with salt and pepper.

Lightly rinse the cucumber, and pat dry. Place in the centre of four warmed shallow pasta bowls and top with the red mullet.

Add the lime juice to the hot sauce, and ladle it around the fish. Top with coriander leaves and serve.

SERVES 4

1 cucumber
2 tsp fine salt
1 tbsp vegetable oil
4 red mullet fillets, around
160 g each
sea salt
freshly ground black pepper
handful of coriander leaves

Sauce:
1 tbsp vegetable oil
1 tbsp curry laksa paste
(eg Reuben Solomon's) or
Thai red curry paste
150 ml chicken stock or water
$\frac{1}{2}$ tsp salt
1 tbsp soft brown sugar
400 ml coconut milk
1 tbsp lime juice

sweet and sour sauce

Sweet and sour fish

If you have been put off sweet-and-sour by the Chinese take-away cliche of glutinous, sickly sweet, crimson sauce, try this sweetly sharp version instead. It is a lot closer to the original Shanghainese recipe, and makes the flavour of the fish jump in your mouth.

SERVES 4

200g bean sprouts

4 tbsp vegetable oil

4 thick white fish fillets
   (eg hake, haddock, cod,
   snapper), around 180g each

2 tbsp cornflour to coat

2 spring onions, finely sliced

Sauce:

6 dried Chinese mushrooms

5cm knob fresh root ginger

2 tsp cornflour

3 tbsp rice vinegar or
   wine vinegar

2 tbsp caster sugar

2 tbsp tomato ketchup

1/2 tsp salt

1 tbsp soy sauce

1 tbsp rice wine or dry sherry

200ml water or chicken stock

Put the dried mushrooms for the sauce in a bowl of boiling water and leave to soak for 30 minutes. Peel and slice the ginger, then cut into very fine matchsticks.

To make the sauce, drain and finely slice the mushrooms, discarding the stems. Mix the cornflour and vinegar to a paste. Place in a small saucepan with the sugar, tomato ketchup, salt, soy sauce, rice wine, water and mushrooms. Bring to the boil, stirring until the sauce is thick and glossy.

Rinse the bean sprouts and shake dry. Heat half the oil in a fry pan. Add the ginger and fry for 1 minute, stirring, then lift out with a slotted spoon and add to the sauce. Fry the bean sprouts in the pan for 30 seconds, then divide among four warmed dinner plates.

Coat the fish fillets lightly with cornflour. Heat the remaining oil in the pan and fry the fish fillets for around 3 minutes on each side until golden. Place on the bean sprouts and spoon the hot sauce over the top. Scatter with spring onions and serve, with rice or noodles.

Salmon, bacon and peas

Salmon is the little black dress of home entertaining, able to be as formal or casual as you like. Swap the peas for a green salad or char-grilled vegetables accordingly.

Wrap each salmon fillet in a rasher of bacon. Finely chop the rest of the bacon and the onion.

Heat half the olive oil in a fry pan and cook the onion for 5 minutes, then add the chopped bacon and cook gently for 10 minutes until the onion is soft and translucent.

Cook the peas in simmering salted water for 5 minutes or until tender. Drain and refresh under cold running water. Drain well and add to the bacon and onion with pepper to taste. Reheat gently.

Heat the remaining oil in a non-stick frying pan and sear the salmon for 2 to 3 minutes on each side until the bacon is crisp and the salmon is still pink in the centre. Spoon the peas and bacon onto warmed plates, top with the salmon and serve.

SERVES 4
4 salmon fillets, around
180 g each
8 rashers rindless streaky
bacon or pancetta
1 onion, peeled
2 tbsp olive oil
450 g podded fresh or
frozen peas
sea salt
freshly ground black pepper

Duck with beetroot

Duck breasts don't have to be undercooked inside and over-scorched outside. Gently steaming them before pan-frying to crisp and colour the skin makes it easy – for both you and the duck to get it right.

Cook the unpeeled beetroot in boiling water until tender – this can take up to 1 hour, but at least you don't have much to do. Drain, reserving 200 ml of the water. Rinse the beetroot under cold running water and rub off the skins and stems, then cut into small dice.

Return the beetroot to the pan. Add the reserved liquid, vinegar, sugar, salt and pepper. Bring to the boil, stirring, and allow to bubble until the liquid is reduced to a slightly sticky syrup. Keep warm.

SERVES 4

4 duck breasts with skin, around 200 g each

½ tsp salt

1 tbsp thyme sprigs

2 tsp olive oil

Beetroot:

4 medium beetroot

50 ml white vinegar

150 g caster sugar

1 tsp salt

½ tsp freshly ground black pepper

Meanwhile, wash and dry the duck breasts, and score the skin in a criss-cross pattern, with a sharp knife. Rub with the salt and thyme leaves. Place on a heatproof plate that will fit into your steamer and steam over simmering water for 20 minutes. Remove the duck breasts and pat dry. (You can prepare to this stage a few hours ahead.)

Heat the oil in a non-stick frying pan and sear the duck breasts, skin-side down, until the skin is crisp and golden. Turn them over, reduce the heat, and cook gently until heated through.

Carve each duck breast thickly on the diagonal, and serve with the beetroot and a leafy green salad.

Rare beef with Thai herbs

The next time you want to 'do something special', go and buy a big, beautiful piece of beef. It's an event, a celebration, and best of all, it rests for an hour before serving so you can do everything in advance. Add a zingy dressing of herbs, chilli, fish sauce and lime juice, and serve it forth to the multitudes.

Place the beef in a shallow dish, rub with the soy sauce and sesame oil, and leave to marinate for a few hours or overnight.

Heat the oven to 220°C/Gas 7. Heat the vegetable oil in a heavy fry pan and sear the beef until browned and crusty all over.

Transfer the seared beef to a lightly oiled roasting tray and roast for 15 minutes. Reduce the setting to 180°C/Gas 4 and cook for a further 25 to 30 minutes, for rare to medium rare. Remove and rest the beef under a loose sheet of foil for an hour before carving.

To make the dressing, whisk the lime juice, fish sauce, sesame oil and sugar together until the sugar has dissolved. Add the shallots, chilli, spring onions and herb leaves, and toss well.

Slice the beef, discarding the string, and arrange on a serving platter. Spoon the dressing over the beef and serve, with lime wedges.

SERVES 6 TO 8
1 kg fillet of beef, rolled
and tied
2 tbsp soy sauce
1 tbsp sesame oil
2 tbsp vegetable oil
2 limes, quartered

Dressing:
2 tbsp lime juice
2 tbsp Thai fish sauce or
soy sauce
1 tbsp sesame oil
2 tsp sugar
4 small red shallots,
finely sliced
1 small red chilli, finely sliced
2 spring onions, finely sliced
handful of basil leaves
handful of mint leaves
handful of coriander leaves

Slashed roast lamb

Lamb slashed almost to the bone cooks faster, remains tender and looks spectacular. You'll end up with chunky slices coated in a garlicky, lemony seasoning that are a joy to eat. Serve with potatoes roasted in the same pan, and a green salad.

Heat oven to 220°C/Gas 7. Holding the leg of lamb with its meatiest side towards you, slash 5 times almost to the bone, at 2.5cm intervals.

Combine the parsley, garlic, anchovies, capers, lemon rind and breadcrumbs in a bowl. Mix in the olive oil to make a paste and push between the lamb slices. Re-shape the meat and tie with string.

Scatter with rosemary, drizzle with a little olive oil and bake for 20 minutes. Reduce setting to 190°C/Gas 5 and bake for another 45 minutes to 1 hour. Leave to rest under foil for 10 minutes.

Strain the juices into a bowl and spoon off surface fat. Remove string and carve across the lamb, parallel to the bone. Arrange on warm plates, drizzle with the juices and serve, with lemon wedges.

SERVES 4 TO 6
1 leg of lamb, around 2kg
3 tbsp roughly chopped parsley
4 garlic cloves, chopped
2 anchovies, chopped
2 tbsp salted capers, rinsed
1 tbsp coarsely grated
lemon rind
4 tbsp soft fresh breadcrumbs
3 tbsp extra virgin olive oil
4 rosemary sprigs
extra olive oil to drizzle
1 lemon, quartered

sweet

Cranberry jelly and cream

This sparkling dessert jelly is made with easily obtainable cranberry juice. Add a splosh of port for those old enough to remember port wine jelly.

In a saucepan, combine the cranberry juice, sugar, and port if using. Heat slowly to just under the boil, stirring to dissolve the sugar. Remove the pan from the heat.

Soak the leaf gelatine in cold water for 3 minutes until blobby, then squeeze out the excess water and whisk the gelatine into the hot cranberry liquid until melted. Or sprinkle the powdered gelatine directly over the hot liquid and leave for 1 minute, then whisk well.

Leave to cool, stirring occasionally. When cool, pour the cranberry liquid into four 150 ml dry martini glasses or jelly moulds and chill in the refrigerator until set.

If set in glasses, trickle a little cream over the top of each jelly until you have a smooth cream 'frosting', then serve. If set in moulds, turn out onto plates and drizzle with the cream.

SERVES 4

700 ml cranberry juice

100 g sugar

50 ml ruby port (optional)

4 sheets of leaf gelatine or
    22 g powdered gelatine

100 ml single cream

Berry mascarpone

My lighter, summery version of tiramisu uses strawberries, raspberries and berry liqueur instead of coffee and cocoa. Like a traditional tiramisu, it goes all cakey, spongey and creamy, as the flavours swell and ripen.

Halve or quarter the strawberries lengthwise and set aside with the raspberries. In a bowl, beat the eggs and sugar together until creamy, then whisk in the mascarpone until smooth.

Mix the liqueur and milk in a shallow bowl. One at a time, dip half the sponge fingers in the liquid, just long enough to coat, and arrange over the base of a large, but not too deep, serving dish.

Cover with a layer of mascarpone cream and scatter with berries. Repeat with another layer of dipped sponge fingers, then mascarpone. Top with a generous layer of berries, allowing some to sink into the cream. Chill for 4 or 5 hours before serving.

Note: this recipe contains raw egg.

SERVES 6

500 g strawberries, hulled

250 g raspberries

3 large free-range eggs

100 g caster sugar

500 g mascarpone

100 ml pink berry liqueur

(eg Framboise)

100 ml milk

200 g Italian sponge fingers

(savoiardi)

lemon posset

Lemon posset

In medieval England, a posset was a sweetened, lightly curdled milk drink. The modern posset is of cream and sugar, acidulated with lemon juice. It's just like a rich, gooey lemon curd without all that mucking around with egg yolks.

Combine the cream and caster sugar in a saucepan and bring to the boil, stirring. Reduce the heat and bubble for 3 minutes, stirring constantly, without allowing the cream to boil over.

SERVES 4

450ml double or whipping
   cream
125g caster sugar
60ml lemon juice

Remove from the heat and add the lemon juice, stirring well. Taste, and add a little more lemon juice if you so desire. Leave the posset to cool for 10 minutes, then stir once more and pour into four 100ml ramekins, Chinese tea cups or espresso coffee cups.

Cool the posset and chill in the refrigerator for a few hours before serving, with tiny spoons.

Pineapple vodka crush

This is so spritzy and refreshing that people put a spoonful in their mouth and immediately go 'wow'. It's great at the end of a barbecue, or after something spicy. And if you put it in the freezer and forget to stir it, don't worry, the vodka prevents it from freezing into a solid block – after 15 minutes in the fridge it will be soft enough to serve.

Cut the top off the pineapple and slice lengthwise into quarters. Slice off and discard the core, then cut the skin and the 'eyes' away from the flesh. Cut the pineapple flesh into cubes.

Whiz the pineapple flesh in a blender with the vodka, sugar, lemon juice and mint leaves.

Pour the mixture into a plastic container or ice-cream tray and freeze for an hour or two until firm on the outside and still liquid in the centre. Tip the mixture into a bowl and beat well, then return to the freezer for another hour or so, until partly frozen. Beat again, breaking up any crystals, then freeze until required.

Chill 4 bowls or glasses, and leave the pineapple crush in the refrigerator for 15 minutes to soften before serving. Scoop into the chilled bowls or glasses and serve, with a sprig of mint on the side.

SERVES 4
1 kg pineapple
100 ml vodka
100 g caster sugar
1 tbsp lemon juice
15 mint leaves
4 mint sprigs

Frozen chocolate mousse

This is better than ice-cream: a rich, creamy, gooey, moussey parfait, ready to slice, chop or scoop. Use a light hand to fold the cream into the chocolate mixture: better to have a few streaks of cream through the mousse than lose all the lightness and volume.

Melt the chocolate in a heatproof bowl set over a pan of gently simmering water, then set aside to cool for 3 minutes.

In a bowl, beat the eggs, egg yolks and sugar together for a few minutes, using a hand-held electric beater, until pale and thick. Add the melted chocolate and beat constantly for about 3 minutes, then stir in the vanilla extract and whisky.

SERVES 6

200g dark, bittersweet
   chocolate, chopped
2 large free-range eggs, plus
   2 egg yolks
100g caster sugar
1 tsp vanilla extract
2 tbsp whisky, Cognac or
   Amaretto liqueur
250ml whipping cream
bitter cocoa powder to dust

In another bowl, beat the cream until it forms light peaks. Fold the cream lightly through the chocolate, then pour into a 1 litre loaf tin. Cover with cling film and freeze overnight.

To serve, soften the mousse in the refrigerator for 15 minutes, or dip the base of the tin very briefly in hot water and run a knife around the edges. Turn out and cut into thick slices or chunks, or scoop straight from the tin. Serve immediately, dusted with cocoa powder.

Note: this recipe contains raw egg.

Simple passionfruit soufflé

Even the biggest scaredy cat can now make a soufflé. This is based on the lightest, tangiest, most beautiful soufflé in the world, that of the revered (and retired) Fredy Girardet of Switzerland. There are no sauces to make and no sorcery to employ – just egg yolks and whites, passionfruit and sugar.

Heat the oven to 200°C/Gas 6. Butter the insides of four small individual soufflé dishes or ramekins, lightly dust each one with 1 tsp sugar, tipping out any excess, and place on a baking tray.

Strain the passionfruit pulp until you have 50 ml juice; discard the seeds. In a bowl, beat the egg yolks with 60 g caster sugar until pale and smooth. Add the passionfruit juice, beating well.

SERVES 4
1 tbsp melted butter
100 g caster sugar, plus 4 tsp
100 ml passionfruit pulp
   (about 4 passionfruit)
3 free-range eggs, separated,
   plus 2 extra egg whites
icing sugar to dust

Whisk the 5 egg whites in a large, clean bowl. Add 20 g sugar and whisk until they start to thicken. Add the remaining sugar and keep whisking until soft peaks form. Gently fold one third of the egg whites into the yolks, then fold in the remainder.

Fill the soufflé dishes to the brim and smooth the tops. Bake just below the middle of the oven for 10 minutes until puffed and golden.

Dust each soufflé with icing sugar, gently place on a serving plate and serve immediately, with cream or ice-cream to one side.

Lemon sugar crêpes

When I was a child, Italian restaurants served a magical dish of hot golden crêpes with lemon juice and sugar. Use granulated sugar for a crunch to contrast with the velvety smooth crêpes.

Blend the flour, sugar, salt, melted butter, whole egg and egg yolk in the food processor. Add the milk gradually, with the motor running, to make a smooth and creamy batter. Rest for at least 30 minutes.

Brush a crêpe pan or small non-stick frying pan with melted butter and place over a medium heat. When hot, add a ladleful of batter and swirl the pan so it covers the base thinly. Cook for a minute or two until the base is lightly golden.

Turn the crêpe over and cook the other side very briefly. Slide onto a warm plate, sprinkle with sugar, and roll into a tight cigar-like cylinder. Cover and keep warm while you do the rest.

Serve two crepês per person on warm plates, sprinkled with extra sugar and lemon juice. Serve with ice-cream and a wedge of lemon.

MAKES 8
Batter:
100 g plain flour
40 g caster sugar
pinch of salt
1 tbsp melted butter
1 free-range egg, plus
1 egg yolk
200 ml milk
extra melted butter to cook

To serve:
2 tbsp granulated sugar
juice of 2 lemons
1 lemon, quartered

fruit

Warm spiced cherries Make a syrup by heating 100g sugar with 200ml water, a squeeze of lemon juice and 4 cloves. Add 300g pitted ripe cherries and gently poach for 2 minutes. Add 2 tbsp cherry or berry liqueur and serve warm with thick cream or a wedge of chocolate cake.

Spicy saffron pears Peel 4 ripe, firm pears and poach in a syrup made by heating 100g sugar with a good pinch of saffron, a few cardamom pods and enough dry white wine to cover. Serve with a dollop of yoghurt and a grind of black pepper.

Caramel apples Peel, quarter and core 4 apples and sizzle in a non-stick fry pan with 2 tbsp butter, 2 tbsp soft brown sugar and 2 tbsp sultanas until golden. Serve with ice-cream or crème fraîche.

Peach and prosciutto Serve a perfect fresh peach with a platter of thinly sliced prosciutto, a wedge of lemon and a generous rocket and parmesan salad for a summer lunch. Or cut the peach into segments and wrap in a short length of prosciutto for nibbles with drinks.

Vineyard sausages Slowly sizzle some well-pricked garlicky pork sausages in a pan, then add a handful of green grapes. Cook until the grapes warm, split, and spill their juices into the pan. Serve the sausages on a rocket salad with the grapey juices spooned over.

Red berry wine Press a punnet of fresh berries through a fine sieve, and stir the juices into 4 glasses of well chilled dessert wine. Add a dash of Cointreau or berry liqueur to sweeten if it tastes too tart.

Red berry meringues Crush two thirds of a punnet of raspberries with a fork, then gently mix with the remaining whole berries. Sandwich 16 crisp little meringues together with 150 ml whipped cream and the berries for a dessert or afternoon tea.

Toffee lime bananas Cut 4 unpeeled bananas in half lengthwise. Sprinkle the cut sides with 4 tsp granulated sugar and place under the grill until the sugar bubbles and browns. Serve the soft bananas with chilled crème fraîche, soured cream or ice-cream and a lime wedge.

Balsamic strawberrries Wash 450g strawberries and hull. Place in a bowl with 2 tbsp balsamic vinegar and a grind of black pepper, toss lightly and leave for an hour before serving. The vinegar and pepper intensify the flavour and tend to disappear into the berries.

Berry swizzlers Thread blueberries, strawberries and raspberries on little bamboo skewers. Dust with icing sugar and serve as a chic dessert with yoghurt for dipping – or use as a swizzle stick in cocktails, fruit punches and fresh fruit smoothies.

Frosted grapes A pretty way to finish a cake, fruit tart or jelly. Frost little bunches of 3 or 4 grapes, by painting the grapes with lightly whisked egg white and gently rolling them in caster sugar.

Sunday roast fruit When next you roast a leg of pork or duckling, cut 4 mandarins or clementines in half and add them to the roasting juices for the last 30 minutes. Serve warm, ready to squeeze over the meat for an instant citrus sauce.

red berry meringues

chocolate pear pudding

Chocolate pear pudding

I like these two-for-the-price-of-one puds. In this lush, gooey chocolate pud, you also get tender baked pears peeking out. If your pears are slightly under-ripe, first poach them in white wine and sugar for 10 minutes.

Heat the oven to 170°C/Gas 3. Beat the butter and sugar together in a bowl until smooth. Add the eggs, one at a time, beating well.

Sift the flour, cocoa powder and baking powder together over the mixture and beat well with a wooden spoon. Add the milk, stirring until smooth. Spoon the mixture into a lightly buttered 30 x 20 cm pie dish or gratin dish and spread evenly.

Peel the pears and cut a 1 cm slice from the base of each one so they will stand upright. Push them firmly into the mixture.

Bake for 30 minutes or until the pudding has puffed up around the pears and set at the edges, but is still a bit gooey in the centre. Serve with cream or crème fraîche.

SERVES 4

125 g butter, melted

200 g caster sugar

3 large free-range eggs

180 g plain flour

75 g cocoa powder

1 tsp baking powder

70 ml milk

4 ripe pears (eg Conference)

Pineapple sushi

No, not sushi as in raw fish, but sushi as in sweet coconut rice topped with fresh tangy pineapple. Fresh mango works beautifully, too. You can pick the sushi up and eat them in your fingers, or serve with a dessert knife and fork.

Put the rice, sugar, coconut milk and water in a saucepan, and bring to the boil, stirring constantly to prevent sticking. Simmer very gently, uncovered, on the lowest possible heat for 20 minutes; stir occasionally, and keep an eye on it to avoid any boiling over.

Once the rice has absorbed the liquid but is not yet cooked, cover the pan tightly and leave over the same gentle heat for another 10 minutes until the rice is tender.

Lightly rinse out a 20 x 15 cm shallow tin or pie dish. Tip in the rice and spread it out evenly, to a 2 cm depth. Smooth the top and leave to cool. Cover with cling film and chill for an hour or two.

When chilled, cut the rice into fingers, about 3 x 8 cm. Trim the pineapple flesh into matching oblongs, and place on top. Serve one or two sushi fingers per person.

MAKES 12
300 g sushi rice
100 g caster sugar
200 ml canned coconut milk
400 ml water
500 g peeled, cored fresh pineapple

Banana bread

This cake-like banana bread will stay moist for several days of breakfasts, brunches, afternoon teas, and I'll-just-have-a-small-slice-before-bed moments.

Heat the oven to 180°C / Gas 4. Lightly butter a 25 x 10 cm loaf tin. Sift the flour, baking powder and salt into a bowl; set aside. Mash the bananas to a purée.

Cream the butter and sugar together in a bowl, with a hand-held electric beater, until smooth and pale. Add the eggs one at a time, beating well until just combined.

Fold in the mashed bananas, vanilla and walnuts, using a spatula, then lightly fold in the flour. Spoon the mixture into the loaf tin.

Bake for 1 hour or until a skewer inserted in the middle comes out dry, covering the top with foil if it starts to brown too quickly. Allow to cool in the tin for 20 minutes before turning out. Serve warm or at room temperature, cut into thick slices.

SERVES 6

250g plain flour

2 tsp baking powder

pinch of salt

3 ripe bananas, around 450g

125g butter, softened

150g caster sugar

2 large free-range eggs

$\frac{1}{2}$ tsp vanilla extract

50g walnuts, chopped

Little berry cakes

To do these as chic little petits fours, you will need a 24-hole mini-muffin or petits four tray. Otherwise, call them not-so-little berry cakes and bake them in a standard 12-hole muffin tray.

Heat the oven to 170°C/Gas 3. Lightly butter a tray of 12 muffin moulds or 24 mini moulds or line with the appropriate paper cases.

Using an electric mixer, beat the softened butter and sugar together until smooth. Beat in the eggs, one at a time. Sift in the flour and salt, and fold through until well mixed. Finally, stir in the milk and vanilla until smooth.

Spoon the batter into the moulds. Drop a single berry on top of each little cake; place three on muffin-sized cakes.

Bake little cakes for 12 to 15 minutes, larger ones for 18 to 20 minutes, or until a skewer inserted in the centre comes out clean.

Cool to room temperature, dust with icing sugar and serve.

MAKES 12 OR 24
125g butter, softened
125g caster sugar
3 large free-range eggs
180g self-raising flour
pinch of salt
60ml milk
1/2 tsp vanilla extract
24–36 raspberries or
blueberries
icing sugar to dust

Chocolate cup cakes

Cakes made with cocoa powder are lighter than those made with chocolate. I take this to mean you can eat more of them.

Heat the oven to 180°C/Gas 4. Arrange 12 paper muffin or cup cake cases in a muffin tray.

Using an electric mixer, beat the softened butter and sugar together until smooth. Beat in the eggs, one at a time. Sift in the flour and cocoa powder, and fold through the mixture until well mixed.

Spoon the mixture into the cases and bake for 15 to 20 minutes until the tops spring back to the touch. Leave in the muffin tray for 5 minutes, then transfer to a wire rack to cool completely.

Dust the cup cakes with icing sugar. Or to make the icing, melt the chocolate and butter in a heatproof bowl over simmering water, stir until smooth, then cool for 5 to 10 minutes to thicken. Spread each cup cake with icing, and sprinkle with gold leaf. Leave to set.

MAKES 12
150g butter, softened
200g caster sugar
4 large free-range eggs
150g self-raising flour
50g bitter cocoa powder
icing sugar to dust

Chocolate icing:
50g dark, bitter chocolate, chopped
50g butter
edible gold leaf sprinkles (from cake decorating specialists)

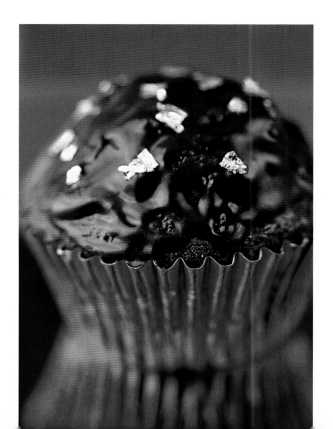

recipe index

index

conversions

volume

5 ml	1 teaspoon (tsp)
10 ml	1 dessertspoon (dsp)
15 ml	1 tablespoon (tbsp)
20 ml	1 Australian tablespoon
30 ml	1 fl oz
40 ml	$1^{1}/_{2}$ fl oz
55 ml	2 fl oz
70 ml	$2^{1}/_{2}$ fl oz
85 ml	3 fl oz
90 ml	$3^{1}/_{2}$ fl oz
100 ml	$3^{3}/_{4}$ fl oz
115 ml	4 fl oz
125 ml	$4^{1}/_{2}$ fl oz
140 ml	5 fl oz
155 ml	$5^{1}/_{2}$ fl oz
170 ml	6 fl oz
185 ml	$6^{1}/_{2}$ fl oz
200 ml	7 fl oz
225 ml	8 fl oz
240 ml	$8^{1}/_{2}$ fl oz
255 ml	9 fl oz
285 ml	10 fl oz ($^{1}/_{2}$ pint)
350 ml	12 fl oz
375 ml	13 fl oz
400 ml	14 fl oz
425 ml	15 fl oz ($^{3}/_{4}$ pint)
450 ml	16 fl oz
565 ml	20 fl oz (1 pint)
710 ml	25 fl oz ($1^{1}/_{4}$ pints)
850 ml	30 fl oz ($1^{1}/_{2}$ pints)
1 litre	35 fl oz ($1^{3}/_{4}$ pints)
1.2 litres	2 pints

weight

7.5 g	$^{1}/_{4}$ oz
15 g	$^{1}/_{2}$ oz
20 g	$^{3}/_{4}$ oz
30 g	1 oz
40 g	$1^{1}/_{2}$ oz
55 g	2 oz
70 g	$2^{1}/_{2}$ oz
85 g	3 oz
90 g	$3^{1}/_{2}$ oz
115 g	4 oz
125 g	$4^{1}/_{2}$ oz
140 g	5 oz
170 g	6 oz
200 g	7 oz
225 g	8 oz
255 g	9 oz
285 g	10 oz
310 g	11 oz
340 g	12 oz
370 g	13 oz
400 g	14 oz
425 g	15 oz
455 g	1 lb
500 g	1 lb 2 oz
565 g	1 lb 4 oz
600 g	1 lb 5 oz
680 g	1 lb 8 oz
700 g	1 lb 9 oz
750 g	1 lb 10 oz
800 g	1 lb 12 oz
905 g	2 lb
1 kg	2 lb 3 oz

length

5 mm	$^{1}/_{4}$ inch
1 cm	$^{1}/_{2}$ inch
2.5 cm	1 inch
5 cm	2 inch
7.5 cm	3 inch
10 cm	4 inch
12 cm	5 inch
15 cm	6 inch
18 cm	7 inch
20 cm	8 inch
23 cm	9 inch
25 cm	10 inch
28 cm	11 inch
30 cm	12 inch

oven temperatures

140°C	275°F	Gas 1	Cool
150°C	300°F	Gas 2	Slow
170°C	325°F	Gas 3	Moderately slow
180°C	350°F	Gas 4	Moderate
200°C	400°F	Gas 6	Hot
220°C	425°F	Gas 7	Hot
230°C	450°F	Gas 8	Very hot